POLITICAL EXCHANGE AND PUBLIC POLICY

POLITICAL EXCHANGE AND PUBLIC POLICY

A CROSS-NATIONAL ANALYSIS

PRAKASH SARANGI

CONCEPT PUBLISHING COMPANY, NEW DELHI-110059

ISBN 81-7022-242-7

First Published 1990

Prakash **Sarangi** (*b.* 1954)

Published by
Ashok Kumar Mittal
Concept Publishing Company
A/15-16, Commercial Block, Mohan Garden
NEW DELHI - 110059 (India)

Lasertypeset by
Microtech Advance Printing Systems (Pvt.) Ltd.
H-13, Bali Nagar
NEW DELHI - 110015

Printed in India by
Taj Press
DELHI-110006

CONTENTS

List of Tables 6
List of Figures 6
Acknowledgements 7

1. Introduction 9

2. Monopolistic Political Competition Implications For Policy Change 28

3. A Cross-National Empirical Analysis 54

4. Conclusion 83

Appendices
- A. Lost of Variables 90
- B. The Data 91
- C. Correlation Matrix of the Variables 97
- D. Mean, Standard Deviation Minimum and Maximum Values of the Variables 98

Bibliography 99
Index 107

LIST OF TABLES

		Page
2.1	Median Voter's Benefits and Costs (in $) from a Hypothetical Policy	38
3.1	Changes in Transfers	67
3.2	Changes in Direct Taxes	68
3.3	Changes in Transfers and Direct Taxes	74

LIST OF FIGURES

2.1	Policy Benefit Function	40
2.2.	Policy Cost Function	41
2.3.	Success Maximization of a Policy	44
2.4.	Minimizing the Failures of a Policy	50

ACKNOWLEDGMENTS

THIS monograph is a revised version of the dissertation which I had submitted to the University of Rochester for the degree of Doctor of Philosophy. My greatest debt, therefore, is to my supervisors, Professors William H. Riker and G. Bingham Powell, Jr. Prof. Riker introduced me to the rational choice approach and its significance in the political inquiry. Prof. Powell taught me the basics of comparative approach and inspired me to undertake cross-national analysis. Both of them provided invaluable comments on the preliminary drafts. Others who have directly or indirectly helped me in shaping of my ideas are: Larry Bartels, William Bluhm, Bruce Bueno de Mesquita, Gerry Bushee, David Castle, Larry Evans, Paul Gehman, Eric Hanushek, Jeff Hill, Grace Iusi, Dave Lalman, Richard Niemi, Lynda Powell, Harold Stanley, David Weimer and Michael Wolkoff. None of them, of course, bears any responsibility for the shortcomings of this study.

Ministry of Human Resources Development of the Government of India awarded me a fellowship which made the trip to USA possible. Utkal University, where I worked as a lecturer during the period, granted me study leave. University of Hyderabad provided me with a generous financial assistance to publish this monograph. I am grateful to all these institutions.

Last, but most important, I thank Gitu and Seema for providing me with the comforts of a home in Rochester while most parts of this work was done.

Prakash Sarangi

ONE

INTRODUCTION

IN a political system we notice frequent changes in public policies ranging from minor changes in an existing policy to its total abandonment. In a stable political environment, even a minor change in a public policy may have far reaching implications. In the short run it may affect the benefits of a particular section of the population or increase a citizen's tax share; and in the long run it may change the demographic characteristics of the country or increase dependence on foreign countries. There is a great deal of dispute among political theorists on whether policy makers or policy takers benefit out of such changes. In a non-democratic system, one may be tempted to dismiss the problem by explaining the changes as the imposition of the will of a dictator or of an ideology. But in the case of a democratic system, such changes may be either a reflection of the demands of the people or a conscious attempt by the incumbent party to arrive at a policy best suited to its interests.[1] The interests of the incumbent party has to act according to the peoples' choices in order to remain in power for more than one term. The present decision makers have to compete with future aspirants. While making policy decisions,[2] they will be guided not by what the people as a whole want, but what they perceive to be the needs of their future supporters.

Policy analysts who look for reasons for a policy change try to find the impact of political or economic environments on a policy. They hardly notice that public policy is often utilized by the policy makers as an instrument to induce policy takers to vote for them at the next election. It is a remarkable feature of politics that the policy-makers have all the state's (unlimited!) resources at their disposal to manipulate and to provide incentives to their own supporters. Thus, changes in a policy reflects a process of exchange between the incumbent party[3] and its future supporters. Benefits (or costs) from public policies are exchanged for support (or opposition) for the policies. I call this process 'political exchange' and the purpose of this monograph is to theorize about it. But first, let me provide an overview of several other explanations of policy change in the field of comparative policy analysis.

Determinants of Policy: Competing Paradigms

Some years ago two scholars considered the science of comparative politics to be in a preparadigmatic stage.[4] Kuhn describes this stage of the development of science as one characterized by much "random fact gathering" which "in the absence of reason for seeking some particular form of recondite information . . . is usually restricted to the wealth of data that lie readily at hand".[5] Such characterization is perfectly applicable to comparative policy analysis today.[6] This branch of comparative politics is less than two decades old and has a long way to go before it is regarded as 'normal' scientific research. For now, one has to simply identify several competing paradigms in the field. Policy analysis is concerned with three separate but interrelated tasks: describing policy, determining its causes and assessing its consequences. In this study I am concerned with only the second aspect of policy analysis: the determinants of public policy or learning why governments do what they do.[7] I will examine three different explanations of such determinants.

"Political Environment Matters" Hypothesis

One group of scholars attributes the observed variance in public policy outcome to political factors. Such factors include the degree of political institutionalization,[8] the extent of political centralization,[9] the influence of labour unions and socialist parties,[10] the varied potential of interest groups and political parties to articulate and aggregate interests,[11] etc. Some of the earliest systematic comparative studies in this paradigm were undertaken in the field of American state governments. The early works of Key, Lockard, Fenton and others asserted the centrality of the variables representing the characteristics of the state political systems in explaining the policy making.[12]

In cross-national research, Anthony King finds ideology to be the most important policy determinant.[13] His principal argument is that ideas, especially ideas of those who govern, have decisive political, social and economic consequences. There are some scholars who have focused on the pivotal role played by the national political elites in setting the policy agenda and deciding policy outcomes.[14] There are other policy analysts who have tried to reformulate group theory in terms of corporatism and tried to assess economic policy making linkages among the government, business and labour representatives.[15]

Within this paradigm, there are some studies which suggest the importance of organizational and bureaucratic factors as policy determinants. Ashford strongly argues that the organisation of institutionalized power — or more abstractly 'the state' — is the most important determinant of policy outcomes.[16] Other scholars, who are known as 'incrementalists' argue that policy changes only marginally over time, due to the significant impact of bureaucratic organizations and the behaviour of decision makers within them.[17] Such analysis is based on the assumption that, in industrialized nations, responsibility for the formulation and implementation of public policy has increasingly devolved to bureaucratic organizations.[18] This assumption is supported by Heclo's and Schmitter's works:[19] They argue that differences in bureaucratic structure account, in large part, for cross-national differences in policy outputs and in the policy process structure. Decisions makers do not annually review the range of existing and proposed policies, identify societal goals or research the benefits and costs of alternative policies in achieving these goals. They reduce their task by considering only increments of change proposed for next year in programmes or policies. The incrementalists' approach forms a fine link between the 'political environment matters' hypothesis and the 'economics resources model' to be discussed in the next section. To say that public policies this year are related to public policies last year does not contradict the statement that public policies this year and last year are a product of political forces. Both explanations are logically correct.

The Economic Resource Model

The main contention of this approach is that public policy outcomes are largely determined by socio-economic factors and that political factors are largely irrelevant. Several scholars with very divergent intellectual premises have arrived at such a conclusion. It is suggested that there is a logic of industrialism in which the availability of economic resources in countries with rapid economic growth override political factors making for diversity, and progressively shape social structures and public policies in a similar mould.[20] As in the case of the political environment matters hypothesis, the first evidences of empirical justification for this paradigm came from several researches in American state policies which found in general that economic resources were more influential in shaping policies than the political variables.[21] This was later confirmed in the cross-national analyses as well. Jackman finds that governments of wealthier countries allocate more expenditures to meet social needs, which in turn affects the equality of the distribution of income.[22] Wilensky reports that a country's economic growth and its demographic and bureaucratic outcomes are the root causes of the general emergence of the welfare state.[23] Cameron finds that openness of the economy contributes to the expansion of the public economy by facilitating the development of the social infrastructure upon which the Social Democratic and the Labour party electoral support rests.[24] One study even demonstrated that there is little consistent difference (education being one major exception) in expenditure output between capitalist and communist nations along a large number of policy dimensions.[25]

Both the political and economic determinants of policy are essentially explanations based on the general systems approach. However, the political systems do not make policies, policy makers do. Beyond a certain point, the question is not what demands exist and what resources are provided, but what the policy makers make of them. As one scholar explains:[26]

> [The systems] model presumes that the grosser structural and environmental characteristics 'result' in policy outcomes. The adherents argue the parsimony of

the model, that it does not have to enter the muddy waters of human motivation, intention and cognition. However, it also reduces politics to pure mechanism. The system 'responds' to inputs by creating outputs. The policy makers themselves are mute and passive. The assumptions, whether intentionally or not, are deterministic. Politics as a human activity does not enter into the calculus. Politics as a question of public choice is not accounted for.

One has to also remember that the bulk of theorizing about the role of politics or economic resources has not really regarded them as directly causative but facilitative.[27] Politics is not viewed as having direct effects on policy, but as affecting the relationship between demands and policies. Politics is a necessary condition for this relationship to exist. But it is not a sufficient condition for such a relationship, for the working of this process may not act on certain demands. Similarly, economic resources are also largely facilitators and constrainers. The ability of a society to create policies requiring expenditures is heavily contingent upon the societal wealth available. Wealth makes it possible to create a relationship between desires of public policy and that policy. It is a means to achieve some desired end, and not the cause of that end.

Thus neither of these two paradigms really 'explain' the patterns of public policies that occur in democratic governments. One has to take into account not only the choices of the decision-makers, but also the government must be understood as one of the major economic institutions of society and that behaves like more familiar economic institutions — the household and the firm — though the market it confronts is a market for policies rather than goods and services. The rational choice approach is an attempt to solve some of these 'puzzles'.

Rational Choice Approach

This approach posits a set of rational individual political actors and a set of equilibrating conditions under which the policy outcomes are determinate. One moves away from explanations based on systems and environments towards those based on individuals. Instead of resorting to political system characteristics to explain policies, one looks for specific sanctions and incentives that produce the rationale for individual behaviour as the source of policy outcomes. The assumption that "man is a rational, goal-seeking, value maximizing or satisfieing being is one that escapes socio-psychological and cultural bounds on the validity of theory. Giving this assumption content does require knowledge of specific cultures, environmental contexts, but this is a basis for a theory that is genuinely comparative, universal".[28]

The rational choice approach has been employed in various ways to explain policy outcomes. One way is to regard public policies as the translation of individual preferences into collective or political choices. Wade and Curry succinctly summarize the approach thus:[29]

> Institutions and the authority of government may be considered normatively to have their sources in the desires of individual citizens for maximum personal gains at minimum personal costs. Rational men with equal influence in the decisions of society will, when confronted with certain common and unavoidable problems, agree to their own coercion. Only by doing so can they secure the benefits available through collective action, while insuring an equitable distribution of costs. Government is the consequence. It is through the in-

> stitutions of government that collective activity is organized, that social needs are ranked authoritatively, and that costs and benefits associated with public choices are allocated . . . . A society of free, rational and politically equal citizens will choose to establish a political system that translates, as efficiently and effectively as possible, the individual preference into public policy.

The above approach, however, is highly idealistic and can perhaps be utilized only in the restricted cases of small communities where some form of direct democracy prevails. In such a situation each individual is regarded as both demander and supplier of public policies. In the case of a representative democracy, on the contrary, individuals are specialized either as demanders or as suppliers. Students of public policies have generated an array of internally consistent models of public demand[30] and supply[31] resulting in collective choice. In case of the former, one could take the preferences of the political leaders as given and focus attention upon changes in the preferences of private citizens and, therefore, upon the demands made upon the resources available to political leaders. These demanders want a variety of government services and are prepared to pay a certain price for them.[32] In the traditional literature of public finance, it is assumed that this price consists exclusively of the payment of collective costs in the form of taxes. There are, however, a number of government services which are not financed from taxes (e.g., an expansive government policy in a period of economic depression), and there are many voters who contribute little or nothing to collective costs, yet continue to be demanders. However, the price which the demanders pay in all cases is to give political support to certain politicians or political parties. Such support is expressed by "voting for the representatives or on referenda, and by less formal 'civic' action which may range from angry letters and personal campaigns to lobbying and outright bribery".[33]

On the supply side, one could take the conditions imposed upon political leaders as given and focus attention upon their personal abilities and preferences. In that case, policy decisions are expected to vary with the changes in leaders and changes in leaders' preferences. Political leaders are interested in maximizing their own personal utility functions. However, they are subject to the influence of the public and to a set of external resource constraints. To the extent that the public's preferences conflict with those of the political leaders (if the preferences do not conflict, either the political leaders' or the public's preferences can be ignored), the leaders will pursue their own interests subject to the limits of the constraints imposed by the public.[34] During the election, the supply side can be seen in the form of policy proposals which are presented to the voters alongside those of competing candidates.

Political Exchange as a Paradigm

The rational choice approach has a distinct edge over the political or the economic environments hypotheses because of its emphasis on the explanations based on the preferences of individuals. However, it has some deficiencies as well. This study is an attempt to avoid some of these deficiencies while still using the basics of the rational choice approach. First, by regarding policy outcomes as the product of choices of only the demanders or only the suppliers of policies, one is telling only half of the story, at least in the cases of representative democratic systems.

The choices of both of these groups are so interdependent that one can conceivably regard all of them as political actors participating in the decision making process.[35] The political actors may be usefully classified as policy makers and policy takers. All political actors are individuals, although they may act for, or in the name of, a group. Policy outcomes may be regarded as the result of a system of interactions or *exchange* decisions among political actors. An individual has to give up something in order to get something. The thing given up is a *cost* and the thing obtained is a *benefit*. Since every individual has limited resources, the problem for him is to allocate his resources in such a way as to reach the most preferred position. One has to balance what he can get against what he has to forgo in order to get it. Thus there are two elements involved in any exchange decision:

(i) How much of benefit, available at a given cost, does one want?
(ii) How much is one willing to give up in order to get it?

Both questions must be answered by policy-makers as well as by policy takers. Decision by each of the political actors leads to a complex interaction or exchange process between policy-makers and policy takers resulting in a policy outcome.

The political exchange process outlined above clearly departs from that part of contemporary political theory in which political systems are viewed as the result of shared beliefs, aspirations and values. It attempts to explain why available economic resources are utilized in the policy making in the way they are, that is, a policy has a specific outcome not only because resources are available but because the resources are utilized by the incumbent policy makers to placate enough voters for their re-election. "Governments want support, compliance, and resources, while the individual citizens want to improve their shares of the benefits and/or reduce costs. All these individual choices and activities are products of *interdependent choices,* since one person's choice must take uncertain choices of others into account".[36]

The conception of policy determination as essentially an exchange phenomenon is not totally different from an economic exchange. "Political man is not a derivative of economic man, but the same person faced with divergent conditions of choice. Decision rules differ; not human nature".[37] Differences in such decision rules, however, results in several distinctions between the two types of exchange *processes*. These are outlined in the next chapter.

Aside from these distinctions in processes, the similarities are noticeable. Like the economic exchange, it is assumed that men have stable tastes and preferences, preferring more to less of the 'good' in question. As in economics, one sees here simplified assumptions in which men find themselves: be it a market in which many buyers compete for homogeneous services or a democratic political system in which parties must compete for votes. And finally, one tries to make more or less rigorous deductions that rational man will adopt given the assumed preferences and environment.[38]

The concept of political exchange has also similarity with theories of social exchange.[39] These theories do not share the axiomatic nature of fundamental postulates of behaviour of an economic man. They are mainly social psychological theories with their starting premises derived from reinforcement and learning theories,[40] though the influence of classical economics is sometimes evident.

Briefly, social exchange theories state the conditions under which different degrees of reciprocity occur and their impact on interpersonal behaviour. "All contacts among men rest on the scheme of giving and returning the equivalence".[41] While the process of political exchange is quite compatible with this broad notion of social exchange, it does not conform to the latter's expectation of justice, fair exchange or imputations of morality in exchange. In the political process, one political actor may threaten or bribe another political actor in order to get his most preferred outcome. One does not have to impute any moral connotation to such actions.

A second problem with the rational choice approach is that it ignores the institutional mechanisms which help in shaping the choices of individual political actors. Irrespective of whether the choices of the policy makers or of the policy takers result in the policy outcome, the literature of social choice theory indicates that predicting the outcomes by simple amalgamation of individual choices is highly improbable.[42] Riker argues that "prudence in research directs the science of politics towards the investigation of empirical regularities in institutions".[43] The emphasis in the policy analysis has shifted considerably from the methodological individualism of an earlier era of behaviouralism, when social outcomes were explained on the basis of choices, tastes and values of individual voters and legislators. The emphasis now is on the consequence of specific structures and decision rules (majority rule, decentralization, inter-organizational communication, etc.) on policy outputs.[44] Tastes and preferences are still important, but they are analysed as a consequence as well as a cause of particular political structures. If preferences and outcomes diverge, of course, a system or subsystem is likely to be unstable and changes in either preferences or institutions may be attempted to bring it back to equilibrium.

While elaborating the process of political exchange in the next chapter, I will place special emphasis on two institutions which are very important in the democratic political process: the political parties and periodic elections. A political party is equivalent to a firm in the economic sense. For the policy takers, it represents an organization of policy makers and is often associated with some pattern of policy outcome. An election provides the basis of the structure of a political market. In most policy studies using the rational choice approach, the role of *periodic* elections is underemphasized resulting in a description of the political market structure as either monopolistic or competitive. I will show in the next chapter that neither approach is realistic and that the market structure is rather like monopolistic competition.

Generally, the theories which use the rational choice approach have a natural tendency to take a hypothetico-deductive form. However, the models are supposed to be more than a logical scheme for interpreting empirical results.[45] Implications derived from a fairly standard set of assumptions are supposed to be cumulative and conducive to extensions and refinement by other researchers by testing them with available data. Unfortunately, there has not been a single study, to my knowledge, which utilizes genuinely comparative data to test any propositions about the determinants of public policy derived from a rational choice model. It is true that it is difficult to obtain individual level data from several countries. But one can always deduce from the assumptions some testable propositions of aggregative nature about the policy outcomes. I presume that there has been no testing of theories because of a lack of communication between theoreticians and empiricists. I believe that such testing of propositions derived from a deductive theory with cross-national data is possible, in spite of the problems like measurement and specification that a scholar faces.

In the next chapter, I will develop a theory of political exchange pertaining to policy making. Several propositions will be deductively derived from assumptions regarding the preferences of the policy makers and the policy takers and the nature of linkage between the two groups of individuals. In the literatures of policy analysis, there have been attempts to discern the nature of exchange relationship between these two groups of individuals.[46] All these studies, however, have been based on only the empirical data and provide no theoretical explanations of a political exchange relationship. In this dissertation I will provide theoretical explanations of the process of political exchange and will substantiate these arguments with empirical data. In chapter 3, I will test the propositions about the determinants of policy change developed in chapter 2 by using aggregate data from 21 contemporary democratic regimes between 1952-1980. I will also test the explanatory power of these exchange variables with two other competing paradigms: the impact of political environments and the economic explanations.

NOTES

1. Marshall puts it nicely when he says, "We might as reasonably dispute whether it is the upper or the under blade of a pair of scissors that cuts a piece of paper, as whether value is governed by utility or cost of production", quoted from, his *Principles of Economics* in Joan Robinson, *The Economics of Imperfect Competition* (London: Macmillan, 1961), p. 16. The output of public policy is perhaps determined by both the blades of scissors: the peoples' choice and the interests of the policy makers.

2. For the purpose of this study, a policy is defined as a general class of issues facing the incumbent party for a decision which will affect the interests of individuals. The examples of policies are welfare policy, international trade policy, environmental policy, etc. The decision about the rate of unemployment allowance may be an important issue at a particular time or place, but it is a part of the welfare policy of the incumbent party.
3. For convenience, I will use the term in singular throughout this paper, although more than one party might have coalesced to form the government.
4. Robert T. Holt and John M. Richardson, Jr., "Competing Paradigms in Comparative Politics", in Holt and Turner (eds), *The Methodology of Comparative Research* (New York: Free Press, 1970), p. 27.
5. Thomas S. Kuhn, *The Structure of Scientific Revolutions* (Chicago: University of Chicago Press, 1964), p. 64.
6. I am using the term 'comparative policy analysis' in a rather broad sense: wherever *comparative approach* is employed in undertaking a policy analysis. In fact, comparative policy research started with the studies of policies in American States. Similar studies were later undertaken at cross-national level.
7. For good reviews of comparative policy in general, see Douglas Ashford (ed), *Comparing Public Policies: New Concepts and Methods* (Beverly Hills: Sage, 1978); Arthur Cyr and Peter deLeon, "Comparative Policy Analysis", *Policy Sciences*, 6, 1975; Elliot J. Feldman, "Comparative Public Policy: Field or Method", *Comparative Politics*, 10, 1978; M. Donald Hancock, "Comparative Public Policy: An Assessment", in Ada W. Finifter (ed), *Political Science: The State of the Discipline* (Washington, D.C.: APSA, 1983); Howard M. Leichter, "Comparative Public Policy: Problems and Prospects", *Policy Studies Journal*, 5, 1977; B. Guy Peters, "Developments in Comparative Policy Studies: A Brief Review", *ibid.* and Richard Rose, "Comparing Public Policy: An Overview", *European Journal of Political Research*, 1, 1973.
8. Samuel P. Huntington, *Political Order in Changing Societies* (New Haven: Yale University Press, 1968).
9. Harold Wilensky, *The New Corporatism, Centralization and the Welfare State* (Beverly Hills: Sage, 1976).

10. G. Lenski, *Power and Privilege: A Theory of Social Stratification* (New York: McGraw-Hill, 1966).
11. Gabriel Almond and G. Bingham Powell, Jr., *Comparative Politics: System, Process and. Policy* (Boston: Little, Brown, 1978).
12. V.O. Key, Jr., *Southern Politics* (New York: Knopf, 1949); Duane Lockard, *The Politics of State and Local Government* (New York: Macmillan, 1963); John H. Fenton, *People and Parties in Politics* (New York: Scott, Foresman, 1966). Their ideas are supported by empirical evidences in Charles F. Cnudde and Donald J. McCrone, "Party Competition and Welfare Policies in the American States", *American Political Science Review*, 63, 1969.
13. Anthony King, "Ideas, Institutions and the Policies of Governments: A Comparative Analysis", *British Journal of Political Science*, 3, 1973.
14. See, for example, Douglas R. Boulter, "Setting Speed Limits .... and Comparing Public Policy Making", *Comparative Politics*, 13, 1980; and John Higley and Gwen Moore, "Elite Integration in the United States and Australia", *American Political Science Review*, 75, 1981.
15. See, among others, Gerhard Lehmbruch, "Introduction: Neo-Corporatism in Comparative Perspective", in Lehmbruch and Schmitter (eds), *Patterns of Corporatist Policy Making* (Beverly Hills: Sage, 1982).
16. Douglas E. Ashford, "The Structural Analysis of Policy or Institutions Really Do Matter", in his edited, *Comparing Public Policies: New Concepts and Methods* (Beverly Hills: Sage, 1978).
17. See, especially, Charles E. Lindblom, *The Intelligence of Democracy* (New York: Free Press, 1965); and Aaron Wildavsky, *The Politics of Budgetary Process* (Boston: Little, Brown, 1974).
18. Bruce A Williams, "Organizational Determinants of Policy Change", in Thomas R. Dye and Virginia Gray (eds), *The Determinants of Public Policy* (Lexington: D. C. Heath, 1980).
19. Hugh Heclo, *Modern Social Politics in Britain and Sweden* (New Haven: Yale University Press, 1974); Philippe C. Schmitter, "Modes of Interest Intermediation and Model of Societal Change in Western Europe", *Comparative Political Studies*, 10,

1977.

20. See, for example, Clark Kerr, *et al., Industrialism and Industrial Man* (Cambridge: Harvard University Press, 1960); and J. K. Galbraith, *The New Industrial State* (London: Harrish Hamilton, 1967).
21. See, for example, Richard E. Dawson and James A. Robinson, "Inter-Party Competition, Economic Variables and Welfare Policies in American States", *Journal of Politics*, 25, 1963; Thomas Dye, *Politics, Economics and the Public: Policy Outcomes in American States* (Chicago: Rand McNally, 1966); and Richard Winters, "Party Control and Policy Change", *American Journal of Political Science*, 20, 1976.
22. Robert W. Jackman, *Politics and Social Equality* (New York: John Wiley, 1975).
23. Harold Wilensky, *The Welfare State and Equality* (Berkeley: University of California Press, 1975).
24. David R. Cameron, "The Expansion of Public Economy: A Comparative Analysis", *American Political Science Review*, 72, 1978.
25. Fredrick Pryor, *Public Expenditures in Capitalist and Communist Nations* (Homewood: Irwin, 1968).
26. Charles W. Anderson, "System and Strategy in Comparative Policy Analysis: A Plea for Contextual and Experiential Knowledge", in William B. Gwyn and George C. Edwards (eds), *Perspectives in Public Policy Making* (New Orleans: Tulane University, 1975), p. 226.
27. Jeff Stonecash, "Politics, Wealth and Public Policy: The Significance of Political System", in Thomas R. Dye and Virginia Gray (eds), *The Determinants of Public Policy* (Lexington: D.C. Heath, 1980).
28. Roger Benjamin, *The Limits of Politics: Collective Goods and Political Change in Post-Industrial Societies* (Chicago: University of Chicago Press, 1980), p. 4.
29. L. L. Wade and R. L. Curry, Jr., *A Logic of Public Policy: Aspects of Political Economy* (Belmont: Wadsworth, 1970), p. 133.
30. See, for example, Howard Bowen, *Towards Social Economy* (New York: Rinehart, 1948); and Albert Breton, "A Theory of Demand for Public Goods", *Canadian Journal of Economics and Political Science*, Nov., 1966.

31. See, among others, William Niskanen, *Bureauçracy and Representative Government* (Chicago: Aldine, 1971); and Douglas Hartle, *Theory of Budgetary Expenditures* (Toronto: University of Toronto Press, 1977).
32. Hans van den Doel, *Democracy and Welfare Economics* (Cambridge: Cambridge University Press,1979), p. 95.
33. Richard Birdsell, "A Study for the Demand for Public Good", in Richard Musgrave (ed), *Essays in Fiscal Federalism* (Washington, D.C.: The Brookings Institutions, 1965).
34. Fred Thompson and Richard Williams, "A Horse Race Around a Mobius Strip: A review and a Test of Utility–Maximizing and Organizational–Process Models of Public Expenditures", *Policy Sciences*, 11, 1979.
35. R.L. Curry, Jr. and L.L. Wade, *A Theory of Political Exchange: Economic Reasoning in Political Analysis* (Englewood Cliffs: Prentice-Hall, 1968), pp. 1-2.
36. William C. Mitchell, "The Shape of Political Theory to Come: From Political Sociology to Political Economy", *American Behavioural Scientist*, 11, 1967, p. 9.
37. *Ibid*, p. 11.
38. Anthony Heath, *Rational Choice and Social Exchange* (Cambridge: Cambridge University Press, 1976), p. 43.
39. Three very influential works in this area are: George C. Homans, *Social Behavior: Its Elementary Forms* (New York: Harcourt, Brace, 1961); Peter M. Blau, *Exchange and Power in Social Life* New York: Wiley, 1964); and J.W. Thibaut and H.H. Kelley, *The Social Psychology of Groups* (New York: Wiley, 1959). For an attempt to apply their ideas to political situations, See Sidney R. Waldman, "Exchange Theory and Political Analysis", in Andrew Effrat (ed), *Perspectives in Political Sociology* (Indianapolis: Bobbs-Merrill, 1972).
40. J.K. Chadwick-Jones, *Social Exchange Theory: Its Structure and Influence in Social Psychology* (London: Academic Press, 1976).
41. Georg Simmel, *The Sociology of Georg Simmel*, translated and edited by K.H. Wolff (New York: Free Press, 1950), p. 387.
42. For succinct summary of this literature, see William H. Riker, "Implications from Disequilibrium of Majority Rule for the Study of Institutions", in Ordeshook and Shepsle (eds), *Political Equilibrium* (Boston: Kluwer-Nijhoff, 1982).

43. *Ibid*, p. 3.
44. Susan B. Hansen, "Public Policy Analysis: Some Recent Developments and Current Problems" in Ada W. Finifter, *Political Science: The State of the Discipline* (Washington, D.C.: APSA, 1983), p. 224.
45. John P. Blair and Steven M. Maser, "A Reassessment of Axiomatic Models in Policy Studies", in Gordon Tullock and Richard E. Wagner, *Policy Analysis and Deductive Reasoning* (Lexington: D.C. Heath, 1978).
46. See, for example, Douglas A. Hibbs, Jr., "Political Parties and Macroeconomic Policy", *American Political Science Review*, 71, 1977; Francis G. Castles, "The Impact of Parties on Public Expenditure" and Manfred G. Schmidt, "The Role of Parties in Shaping Macroeconomic Policy", both in Castles (ed), *The Impact of Parties: Politics and Policies in Democratic Capitalist States* (Beverly Hills: Sage, 1982); Edward T. Jennings, "Competition, Constituencies and Welfare Policies in American States", *American Political Science Review*, 73, 1979; and Valerie Bunce, *Do New Leaders Make a Difference? Executive Succession and Public Policy Under Capitalism and Socialism* (Princeton: Princeton University Press, 1981).

TWO

MONOPOLISTIC POLITICAL COMPETITION: Implications For Policy Change

SEVERAL years ago Downs stated the highly influential proposition: "parties formulate policies in order to win elections, rather than win elections in order to formulate policies".[1] It is influential not because it is a strikingly simple motivational assumption, but because it changed the way the scholars perceived the role of election in the public policy making. The role of election can be further extended as a fundamental structure, analogous to a market, which facilitates the process of political exchange. In the next section I will explain the rationale of characterizing the structure of political market as monopolistic competition. Then I will present several assumptions of the model. In the subsequent sections the basic model will be presented. At the end I will summarize the several propositions, derived from the model, which provide explanations of policy changes.

The Notion of a Policital Market

Very often the scholars who investigate some form of political market in a democratic system assume the existence of either a purely competitive[2] or a purely monopolistic[3] market structure. In the former approach, the public policy is supposed to reflect the preferences of the majority of voters. The latter approach suggests that there is an element of monopoly power in the hands of policy makers. The legislature, executive, parties or interest groups are able to formulate a policy beyond the level that utility maximizing voters would choose in the absence of a monopoly power. While both of these models are elegant, their assumption of the existence of either a competitive or a monopolistic political market is questionable.

There are four necessary conditions for the existence of a purely competitive market. First, the product (policy) has to be homogeneous. Buyers should think that the units of a product sold by seller *A* are identical to those sold by seller *B* and, as a consequence, have no reason for preferring the output of any one seller over that of any other seller of the product. In the political market, political parties do not advocate identical policies. On the contrary, a party tries to show that its policy is different from others.

Second, each buyer (voter) and each seller (party) of a product (policy) must be so small in relation to the entire market for the product that they cannot significantly influence the price of whatever it is they are buying or selling. In the political market, we can reasonably assume that the influence of each voter is negligible. But influence of a single party on a policy may be very high, particularly if it has a large support base or it is a single issue party, like the Green Party in West Germany. In the period between two elections, the influence of the incumbent party is enormous.

Third, no artificial price restrictions (e.g., governmental price fixing or supply restriction) may be placed on the demand for, the supplies of and the prices of whatever is being exchanged. While producing a public policy, an incumbent party has to face several restrictions, viz., the contractual obligations of the previous governments, dependence on the international environment, etc. On the other hand, the nature of public policy is such that an individual has hardly any choice whether he will accept (consume) a public policy or not. His only choice can be exercised by voting for or against a party at an election.

Fourthly, there should be mobility of goods and services and of resources. New firms must be free to enter any desired industry and resources must be able to secure employment at their highest paid uses. In a political market, new political parties may come into existence or old political parties may change their policies. Voters are free to support or oppose any political party or abstain. While the voters seem to have such a choice, there are a lot of restrictions on the entry of new parties into the political market.[4] Also the political parties do not always make drastic changes in their policies simply to respond to the market demands.

To sum up, in a pure competition with perfect information, the buyers will be paired with the sellers not by their preferences but at random. Such a premise applied to a political situation may seem baffling to many democratic theorists. Equally baffling would be the opposite assumption of a monopolistic market. In a pure monopoly there is supposed to be a single seller of a product for which there are no good substitutes. We cannot dispute the fact that there is no substitute market for a lot of public goods; but there are some areas of policy making which may have substitutes. Education is a typical example. Private schools exist along with the public schools.

The existence of a single policy maker seems also to be implausible. Often the national, state and local governments may be participating in the same or similar areas of policies. At a single level of government one party may have, between elections, the constitutional or legal right to formulate a policy. But it cannot afford to exercise this right to make policy decisions arbitrarily. It would rather carefully watch the policy stance of other potential policy makers, i.e., other competing parties who are temporarily excluded from the policy making process. An incumbent party is usually aware of the fact that its so called monopoly is temporary and that it would have to compete with others at the next election. Thus the assumption of the monopoly market and the theory of representative democracy seem to be incompatible.

Given these constraints, I would rather characterize the structure of the political market as monopolistic competition.[5] It is monopolistic because between two elections one coalition has the quasi-monopoly right to produce public policies. However, the incumbent party's policy decisions may be influenced by the anticipated reaction from its supporters, opponents or even from the anomic behaviour of some groups. In order to win re-election, it has to formulate its policies in such a way that at least a majority of individuals are able to maximize their utilities from these sets of policies compared to any other alternative policies proposed by the opposition parties. This makes the system competitive. The incumbent party is aware that it cannot maintain its monopoly for ever. At election time it has to compete with other coalitions in order to present the best possible bid for the extension of monopoly rights.[6] There is always some probability that one monopoly may be replaced by another monopoly at the election. Thus, characterization of the political market as monopolistic competition seems closer to reality.

Preliminary Assumptions

An individual is a rational, goal seeking and value maximizing being: Following Downs,[7] one can describe a rational individual as one who behaves as follows:

(1) he can always make a decision when confronted with a range of alternatives;
(2) he ranks all the alternatives facing him in order of his preference in such a way that each is either preferred to, indifferent to, or inferior to each other;
(3) his preference ranking is transitive;
(4) he always chooses from among the possible alternatives that which ranks highest in his preference ordering.

A rational individual's goal, in his relations with the government, is to maximize his utility from the output of public policies: Like the *homo economicus* our *homo politicus* calculates the benefits and costs accruing from a public policy while estimating his utility.[8] At an election time, he compares the utility he has derived from *all* the policies of the incumbent party since the last election and the expected utility from any other party if it were given the opportunity to control the government. After such comparison he finds out the party from whom he can expect to obtain maximum utility after the election and votes for that party.[9]

A party's goal is to win an election and thus control the governing apparatus: An incumbent party tries to design public policies in such a way that it can acquire enough support and thus maximize the probability of re-election. Probability of re-election is high if the incumbent party is able to succeed with all or most of its policies.[10] Since there is always uncertainty about the extent of salience of a policy at election time, it should attempt to succeed with each of its policies. Similarly, other parties, while making promises of public policies they will adopt, design their manifestoes in such a way that they can maximize the probability of being elected.

The government has monopoly of formulating and implementing some policies affecting individuals and it is this set of public policies that have vital consequences in the individual's calculus of voting: Some goods and services may be produced both in the public sector and in the private sector. If an individual can choose either a governmental or private supplier, he can switch from one to the other if he is dissatisfied. Hence, the utility derived from the consumption of these goods and services will not be reflected in the individual's decision to vote or not to vote for the incumbent party at the election. He would rather estimate the utilities derived from those policies in which the government has a monopoly. For example, transfer payments or foreign policy decisions come only from the government. Private firms do not compete with the government in these fields.

An individual who is affected by public policies but is indifferent in his opinion about the incumbent party's policies abstains in the election: Public policies may not bring only benefits or only costs. Even benefits or costs may not always outweigh the other. Sometimes an individual neither gains nor loses from the public policies. In such a case, he would be indifferent in his choice between the incumbent party and an opposition party and would abstain from voting in the election.

The policy alternatives are divisible: A policy is never expected to remain static. The unemployment allowance may be increased, decreased or stopped altogether. A policy regarding freedom of speech may be divisible in terms of who is free to speak, in what forum, at what length and on which topics. Thus, the units of a public policy, whether tangible or intangible, can be altered by the incumbent party. "The divisibility of policies enables one to develop the notion of policy 'units', or slices of whatever scope, of policies, and further, enables one to say something about the comparability, the relative evaluation, of policy units. It also enables one to think of public policies as continuous variables; that is, policy or reward variables that can continuously take on new values.[11]

Changes in any single public policy are considered by the incumbent party separately, and not tied to the changes in other public policies: Success of *each* policy which is electorally salient is important for the incumbent party. Therefore, while making a decision about any change in a policy, it will assess the extent to which such changes will contribute to its efforts for re-election, independently of its decisions regarding all other policies.

Nature of Political Exchange

Any policy change involves some form of redistribution of resources. The incumbent party is entrusted with the task of deciding how much, if at all, redistribution will take place. Two major groups emerge among the population as a result: the net beneficiaries and the net losers.[12] What does the incumbent party get from the beneficiaries as a price for its services? If it maintains a particular level of policy output there is some probability of its obtaining support from the gainers. The higher the benefit, the higher the probability of support. The nature of support may be voting in favour of the incumbent party in the next election. There is always, however, some cost of maintaining any level of output. The more an individual loses in benefits, the higher is the probability that he will oppose the incumbent party's policy. Such opposition may be reflected by his voting against the incumbent party in the next election. The individuals try to maximize their expected benefits and minimize their expected costs by voting for the right party. If the incumbent party, by its present policies, fulfils their expectations, they will continue to support it.

The nature of political exchange outlined above is, in some respects, fundamentally different from an exchange in an economic market. First, the political market is coercive in nature. In an economic market, an individual who does not consume potatoes will not have to pay for the cost of production of potatoes. He may not even know anything about their cost of production or the possible benefits that he might derive from them. But an individual in the political market may be compelled to pay taxes to defray additional expenditures because of an environment policy to reduce acid rain, even if he is not affected by the acid rain.

Second, political exchange takes place infrequently and simultaneously. An individual can express his support or opposition towards the incumbent party only at the time of election. Therefore, an individual evaluates his benefits and costs from a policy for a period between two elections and not at a single point of time. Also, the political process requires simultaneous decision about several policies. There cannot possibly be a voting for each policy separately. An incumbent party would like to see all of its policies succeed. But often all policies cannot succeed because one policy may contradict another. A policy to reduce inflation may result in more unemployment. In such cases the party must assess which policy generates the greater support. The role of the incumbent party here is like a corporation that produces several products and is interested in the profits of the corporation as a whole.[13] Although the characteristic of simultaneity complicates the incumbent party's decision calculus, it will try to maximize the profit or minimize the loss in each policy by controlling the level of output so that, in the end, it will obtain the best possible result at the election.

Third, political exchange does not allow unequal privilege to the consumers of public policies. In the economic market, a consumer who likes potatoes will buy more of them compared to his neighbour, even if both might have the same budget constraint. But in the political market, every individual has the same voting privilege, even if some might have greater interest in the public policy decisions. Usually in the economic market every individual does not have the same resource. But in the political market an individual's resource is limited to either zero or one vote. Hence, the incumbent party exchanges the total output of a policy for a total support; but in the economic market one unit of output is exchanged for a price. An individual cannot negotiate to have only one unit of a policy for a partial support. He has to accept or reject the entire package of a policy. It gives the incumbent party the same type of bargaining power as a profit seeking monopoly that discriminates among the customers or that presents the market with an all-or-nothing choice. The primary reason for the differential bargaining power of the incumbent party is the individuals' lack of significant alternatives, at least temporarily, and their unwillingness to forego the services supplied by the incumbent party.

Individual Choice and Public Policy Output

An important aspect of a producer's decision making

process is to study the market. He estimates the number of units he can sell at different levels of prices. In other words he wants to know the value that the individuals are going to attach to his product. Similarly, in a political market, the incumbent party would like to know the amount that the individuals would gain or lose from any of its policies. As noted earlier, unlike the economic market, it would estimate the total benefits or costs that individuals would have at different levels of output. From this it can know the level of output that can be successfully absorbed in the market.

To simplify the process of discovering out this market demand at different levels of output, we can resort to the usual assumption of the decisiveness of the median voter.[15] *The median of the quantity of a policy demanded is the quantity demanded by the median voter:* If this assumption is true, the level of demand for a policy in the market would be the same as the amount desired by the median voter. To be successful, the incumbent party has to formulate a policy so as to bring the median voter's marginal benefit in line with his marginal cost.

A median voter's benefits and costs from a hypothetical policy may look like those in Table 2.1. His total benefit (or the maximum he is willing to pay) for a specific expected level of output is presented in column 2. This relationship between the level of policy output and the total benefit may be termed as policy-benefit function. This function has the following properties: over some range of expected output, the median voter is willing to pay a higher value for a higher expected output. In mathematical terms, the first derivative of this function is positive over the relevant range. Also over some range, the median voter will gain a higher value from an additional unit of output for a smaller expected output than for a larger expected output (column 3). If fewer units are produced it becomes more scarce and hence he will be willing to pay more for getting the benefits. But if a policy is available in abundance and he is pretty sure about getting his share of the policy, he has no incentive to be willing to pay for additional benefits. In other words, the marginal benefit tends to decrease. Thus the second derivative of the function is negative over the relevant range. The median voter's benefits per unit has also a similar relationship (column 4). The per unit policy benefit function has no operational significance for the incumbent party, as it does not offer its services at a price. However, this function, which corresponds to the standard concept of a 'demand' function, is helpful in comparing the behavior of the incumbent party with that of a profit seeking form of organization, since much of the literature on the subject utilizes such a function for the purpose of exposition.

TABLE 2.1: **Median Voter's Benefits and Costs (in $) from a Hypothetical Policy**

Units of a Policy	Total Benefit	Marginal Benefit	Benefits per Unit	Total Cost	Marginal Cost	Cost per Unit
1	2	3	4	5	6	7
1	.24	.24	.24	.06	.06	.06
2	.44	.20	.22	.16	.10	.08
3	.60	.16	.20	.30	.14	.10
4	.72	.12	.18	.48	.18	.12
5	.80	.08	.16	.70	.22	.14
6	.84	.04	.14	.96	.26	.16

The policy-benefit function is also presented in Figure 2.1. As per our assumption, the median voter's policy benefit function would be regarded by the incumbent party as the political system's policy-benefit function. Hence, the curves TB and MB represent the political system's total benefit and marginal benefit from the different levels of policy output. AB, which represents the benefits per unit, may be regarded as the political system's demand curve for the policy. Additionally, it is also the demand curve faced by the incumbent party between two elections, as it is the only producer of public policies.[16] For the reasons outlined in the last paragraph, TB is concave and both MB and AB slope downward to the right.

An individual may benefit from a policy; he may have to incur some costs as well. He may have to pay a special fee to avail the benefits from a policy, his tax share might increase or his more-preferred policy cannot be implemented because of another substitute policy. Because of the universal characteristic of the political exchange, a public policy imposes, potentially, a cost on each and every individual.[17] A typical median voter's total costs (or, the minimum dollars he expects to get back) due to different levels of output of our hypothetical policy may look like column 5 of Table 2.1. This relationship may be called the policy-cost function. This function has the following properties: over some range of expected output, a larger output can be obtained only at a higher cost. The first derivative of this function is always positive. Also a larger output can generally be achieved only with higher costs for an additional unit of output (column 6). Since the incumbent party will have to distribute its total resources among several policy areas, increasing the output of a single policy might deprive the individuals the privilege of obtaining more benefits from another policy. Or, an individual who does not get any benefit from a policy but has to pay his tax share might think that his losses progressively increase as the output of the policy increases.

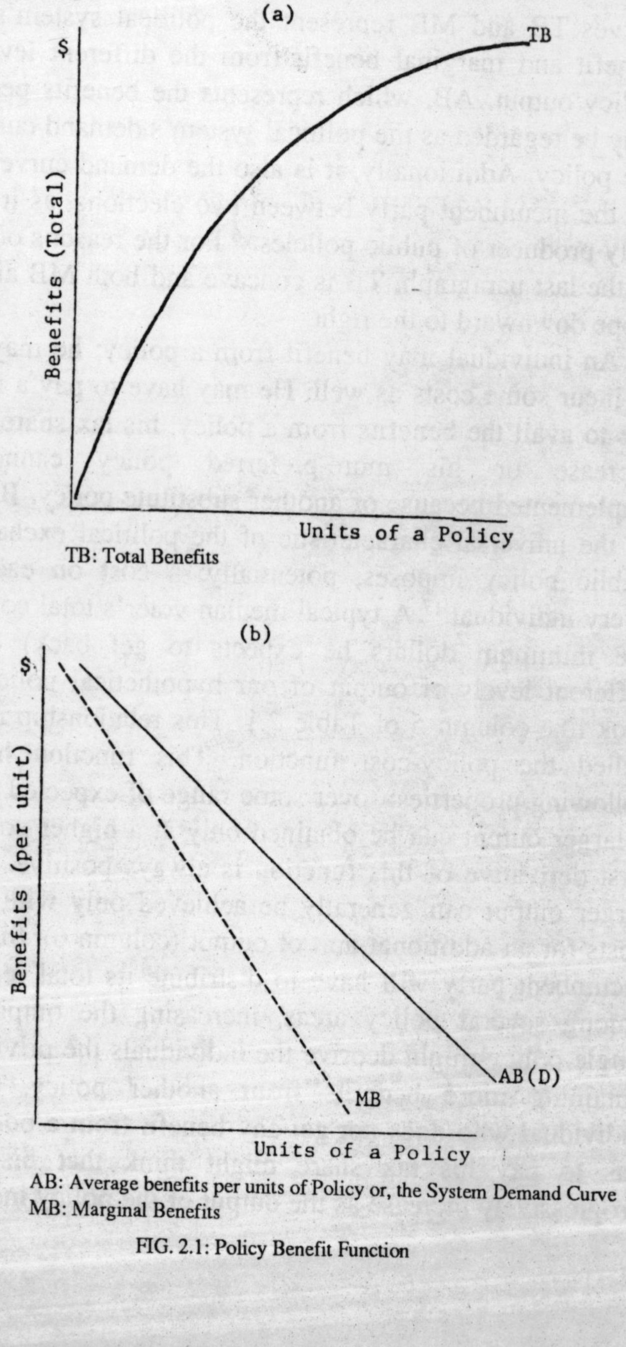

FIG. 2.1: Policy Benefit Function

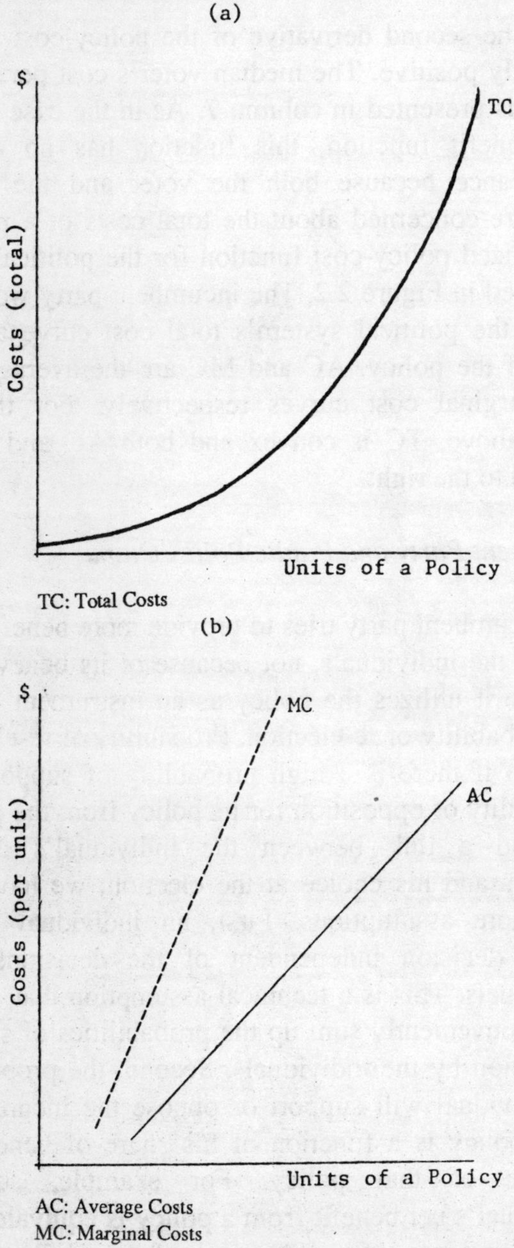

FIG. 2.2: Policy Cost Function

Thus, the second derivative of the policy-cost function is generally positive. The median voter's cost per unit of the policy is presented in column 7. As in the case of the per unit benefit function, this function has no operational significance because both the voter and the incumbent party are concerned about the total costs of a policy. The generalized policy-cost function for the political system is presented in Figure 2.2. The incumbent party would regard TC as the political system's total cost curve at different units of the policy. AC and MC are the average cost and the marginal cost curves respectively. For the reasons given above, TC is convex and both AC and MC slope upward to the right.

Incumbent Party and Public Policy Output

The incumbent party tries to provide more benefits and less cost to the individuals, not because of its benevolence but because it utilizes the policy as an instrument to increase the probability of re-election. Probability of re-election will be high if there is a high probability of support and low probability of opposition for its policy from the population. To find a link between the individual's cost-benefit calculus and his choice at the election, we have to make two more assumptions. First, an individual makes his voting decision independent of the decisions of other individuals. This is a technical assumption that will enable us to conveniently sum up the probabilities of support and opposition by the individuals. Second, the probability that an individual will support or oppose the incumbent party for a policy is a function of his share of benefit or cost because of that policy. For example, suppose an individual's net benefit from a policy is equivalent to eight dollars out of a possible total of ten dollars worth of benefits. We assume that the probability of support for this policy by the individual is 0.8.[18]

An incumbent party, like a profit maximizing firm, would like to maximize the difference between the probability of support and the probability of opposition from the total population. Or, it would like to maximize the difference between the benefits and costs of the median voter from a policy. In our example of the median voter's benefits and costs from a hypothetical policy presented in Table 2.1, the numbers representing his benefits and costs can also be regarded as the probability that he will support or oppose the policy. The generalized policy-benefit function in Fig. 2.1 and the policy-cost function in Figure 2.2 can be renamed as the policy-support function and the policy-opposition function by changing their vertical axes to the probability of support and the probability of opposition in the respective figures. If we follow the arguments outlined earlier in the cases of policy-benefit and policy-cost functions, the total support curve, like the total benefit curve will be concave and the total opposition curve, like the total cost curve will be convex. The marginal support and the average support curves will slope downwards to the right and the marginal opposition and the average opposition curves will slope upwards to the right.

Success for a policy will be maximum when the marginal support (MS) will be equal to the marginal opposition (MO). In Figure 2.3 (a), at an output x, the difference between the total support (TS) and the total opposition (TO) is the greatest. At this output, the slopes of the TS and the TO curves are equal (tangents to the curves at this output are parallel). In the Figure 2.3(b), the level of support that the incumbent party can obtain for each unit of output x is s and the corresponding level of opposition is p. The area *prts* represents the extent of success of the policy.

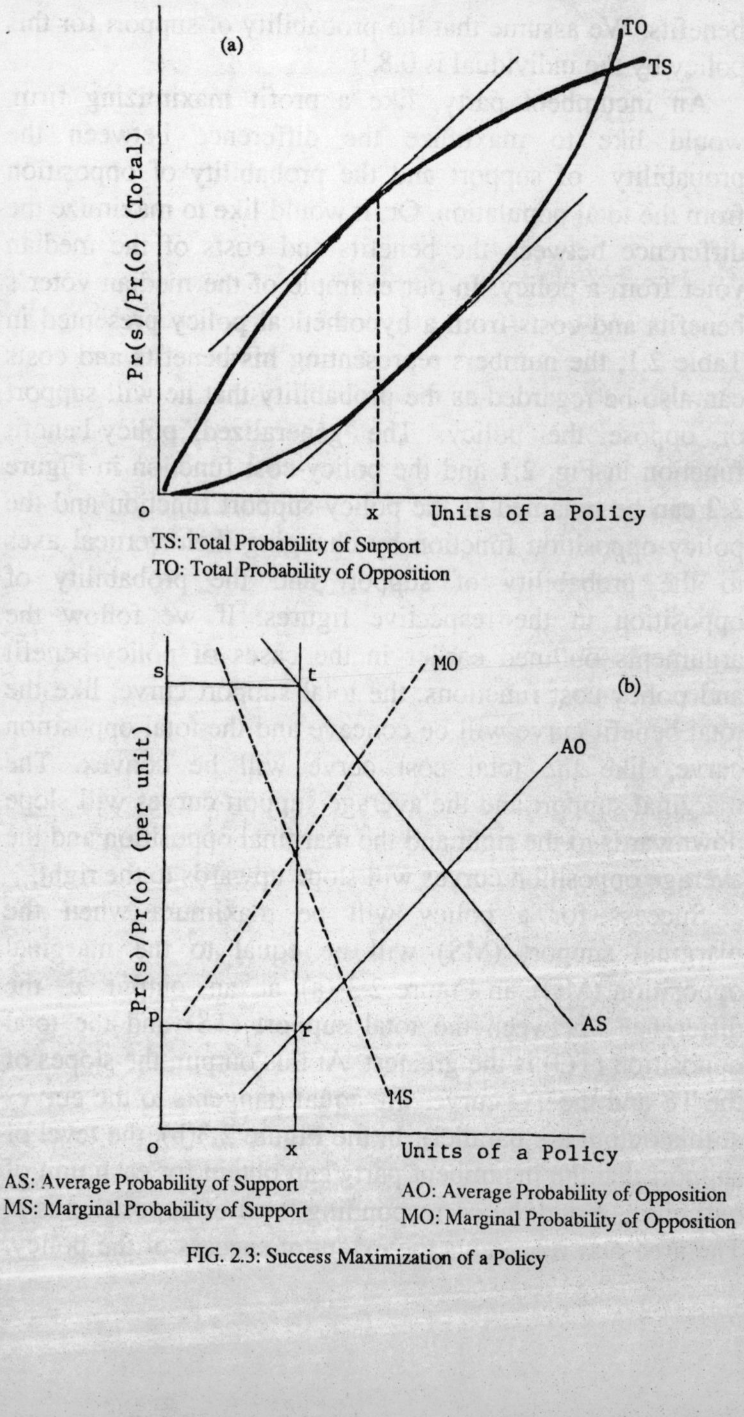

FIG. 2.3: Success Maximization of a Policy

At outputs smaller than *x*, MS is greater than MO. Thus larger output upto *x* add more to total support than to total opposition and increase the probability of success. At larger outputs, MS is less than MO. Hence, increase beyond *x* add more to the total opposition than to toal support and cause the probability of success to decrease. Policy output at the level of *x* units may be termed as equilibrium output. Hence, when the marginal support is equal to the marginal opposition for a policy, there will be no change in the policy output. Or, *there will be no change in the policy output if the marginal benefit of the median voter is equal to his marginal cost due to the policy.* (Proposition 1)

However, the incumbent party is neither interested in maintaining the equilibrium of policy output *per se,* nor it is interested in maximizing the net benefits of individuals. It is interested in maximizing the probability of re-election and thus, maximizing the difference between the number of supporters and opponents. Thus it has to maximize the winning differential D,

$$D = M - N = ms - no \qquad \ldots\ldots\ldots (1)$$

subject to the condition that

$$V = m + n$$
$$s' = o' > O \text{ (proposition 1 and assumption)}$$

where,

M : Total number of voters voting for the incumbent party because of the benefit from the policy.
N : Total number of voters voting against the incumbent party because of the costs of the policy
m : Number of net beneficiaries from the policy
n : Number of the net losers from the policy
s : Probability of support by the net beneficiaries
o : Probability of opposition by the net losers
V : Number of potential voters among the net beneficiaries and the net losers
s′, o′ : first derivatives.

The equation (1) has a very interesting feature. The number of votes in support for the incumbent party depends on m: a larger m provides a broader base for support, but dilutes the net gain per beneficiary and so the probability of support from the beneficiary; similarly, a smaller m may ensure less probability of opposition among losers but a larger size of opponents.

D will be maximized if,

$$(ms)'-(no)' = 0$$

$$\text{or,} \quad (m's)+(s'm)-(n'o)-(o'n) = 0 \qquad \ldots\ldots\ldots(2)$$

We know that m, n, s, o, s′ and o′ are positive and that m′ = —n′. Hence, the only condition on which equation (2) will hold is: m = n. A corollary of this condition is m′ = n′ = 0. Thus the additional condition under which there will be no change in the policy output is: *the net beneficiaries from a policy will be equal to the net losers from the policy.* (Proposition 2) The corollary of this condition is that there will be no marginal change in the beneficiary or the loser groups.

Even if an incumbent party is able to fulfil both of the above conditions of equilibrium, the resulting equilibrium may prevail only in the short run. The success of a policy is actually tested at the time of election. But the incumbent party has to take policy output decisions almost continuously. Moreover, unlike the economic market where the production of a good may be abandoned if the producer sees no signs of profitability, a public policy can rarely be abandoned altogether. In the case where the incumbent party sees no signs of the success of a policy, it may like to maintain an equilibrium output where there is minimization of loss rather than maximization of profit. In the long run, however, if it continues with such a strategy for most of its policies, it will fail to win re-election. In such a case, there will be new coalitions of beneficiares and losers and hence, the existing equilibrium of policy output cannot be maintained.

Policy Output in the Long-run

Success of a policy depends on the relationship between the system demand curve (AS curve in the case of our political market) and the conditions of opposition. Success will be more either if the average support curve shifts upwards or if the average opposition curve shifts downwards. However, the benefits of the beneficiaries or the costs of the losers might have reached such a saturation point that none of these shifts might occur even after repeated changes in policy. For example, if a government's involvement in war is very much disliked by the voters, no minor variation, short of abandonment of the policy of involvement, will be of any help to the incumbent party.

Sometimes the incumbent party may continue to produce a policy, at least in the short-run, knowing very well that it does not succeed in the long-run. Suppose there is an immediate need for providing energy. The government decides to rapidly build several nuclear power plants without, however, ensuring adequate safety standards. In the long-run more people may oppose the policy of having unsafe power plants or the cost of making them safe. In the short-run, however, fewer people will oppose because they get the much needed energy. The incumbent party will continue with that policy, knowing very well the long term failure of its policy, because the average opposition (short run) may be less and it hopes to make some changes in the policy as soon as possible. In such a situation the incumbent party will try to minimize the failures of a policy, i.e., the difference between the total opposition and the total support. In Figure 2.4, the opposition level is so high and the demand for the policy is so low that at no level of output, the AS can cover the AO. The incumbent party is trying to minimize the extent of failure, here *stuv,* but will continue with the policy because the average opposition (short run) is less than the AS for the policy.

In an election, the incumbent party will lose if the AO curve continues to be above the AS curve for most of its policies. As we noted earlier, every election is like a competitive bidding situation. Different parties try to bid for the monopoly right to formulate and implement policies by controlling the government. Any party that can provide the lowest bid (i.e., it can promise to provide public policies which can maximize the utilities of a winning number of individuals) gets the monopoly right for the next term.

Let me assume that the incumbent party is replaced. Let me further assume that the *new* incumbent party wants to continue with a policy that the *old* incumbent party produced resulting in a large opposition. The new incumbent party has two options. It might try to reduce the AO curve to a level below that of the AS curve. Continuing with the earlier example of the construction of nuclear plants, it may assure the opponents that enough safety standards will be maintained at a minimum cost. Or else, it might try to raise the AS curve to a level above the AO curve. It might seek to persuade voters that there were no real safety hazards. If the AO curve shifts, it is very likely that there will be a shift in the MO curve as well, resulting in some change in the output of the policy. Similarly, if the AS curve shifts, it will result in a shift in the MS curve and the consequent change in the output. In either case the new incumbent party cannot continue to produce x units of the policy. Thus, if there is a turnover of the incumbent party at an election, there is a high probability that there will be a change in the units of a public policy output or, *the equilibrium of policy output can be maintained only if an incumbent party is always re-elected.* (Proposition 3)

We have developed three conditions for the existence of an equilibrium in policy output: the median voter's marginal benefit should be equal to his marginal cost; the number of net beneficiaries should be equal to the number of net losers or the marginal change in the beneficiaries should be equal to zero; and there should be no turnover at the election. These are very stringent conditions for a dynamic activity like public policy making. Therefore, in the real world we can expect that we will seldom encounter a policy output in equilibrium. Rather the equilibrium output may be regarded as an ideal output level. The incumbent party always tries to move its policy output in that direction. In other words, if any or all of these conditions are violated, we will observe changes in a policy because the incumbent party would be trying to change the previous output level to move in the direction of equilibrium. Thus, the three conditions for a policy output change are:

(i) the existence of a difference between the median voter's marginal benefit and marginal cost;
(ii) a marginal change in the number of the beneficiaries; and
(iii) a turnover at the election.

Unfortunately the first condition cannot be empirically identified in the absence of the relevant survey data. In order to test for the second condition with the available data, it is necessary to make one more assumption: the marginal change in the number of beneficiaries from a

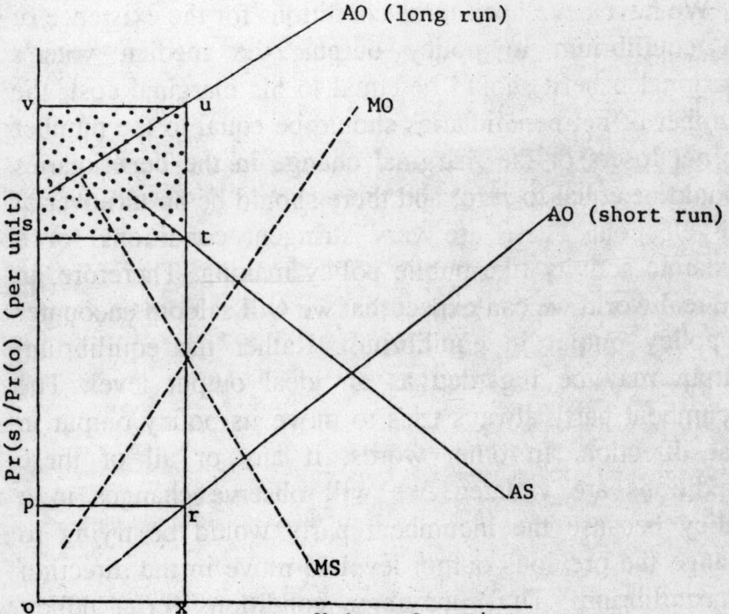

AS: Average Probability of Support
MS: Marginal Probability of Support
AO: Average Probability of Opposition
MO: Marginal Probability of Opposition

FIG. 2.4: Minimizing the Failures of a Policy

policy equals the marginal change in the incumbent party's voting support. In other words, I will use the change in the voting support for a party as an estimate of the change in the number of beneficiaries. This is a reasonable assumption because every incumbent party seeks to provide benefits for its own supporting coalition and any changes in the coalition's strength will be reflected in the changes in the size of the beneficiaries from the policy. In the next chapter I will make a cross-national empirical test for the second and the third conditions.

NOTES

1. Anthony Downs, *An Economic Theory of Democracy* (New York: Harper and Row, 1957), p. 28.
2. See among others, Albert Breton, *The Economic Theory of Representative Government* (Chicago: Aldine, 1974); R.L. Curry, Jr. and L. L. Wade, *A Theory of Political Exchange* (Englewood Cliffs: Prentice-Hall, 1968); and William H. Riker and Peter C. Ordeshook, *An Introduction to Positive Political Theory* (Englewood Cliffs: Prentice-Hall, 1973), pp. 240-271.
3. See among others, W.A. Niskanen, *Bureaucracy and Representative Government* (Chicago: Aldine, 1971); T. Romer and H. Rosenthal, "Political Resource Allocation, Controlled Agendas and Status-quo", *Public Choice,* 33(4), 1978, pp. 27-43; and M. P. Fiorina and R.G. Noll, "Voters, Bureaucrats and Legislators: A Rational Choice Perspective on the Growth of Bureaucracy", *Journal of Public Economics,* 7(2), 1978, pp. 239-254.
4. The rule of five per cent minimum vote in West Germany is illustrative of this. Forfeiture of deposits in many countries is another example. In most countries there is some form of an Election Commission which regulates the entry and exit of political parties. In some plurality voting systems, the system itself restricts entry endogenously.
5. Although I use the same terminology, its meaning is different from E. H. Chamberlin's *Theory of Monopolistic Competition,*

8th Ed. (Cambridge: Harvard Univ. Press, 1962). Chamberlin assumes the existence of several sellers with differentiated products.

6. This is like a competitive bidding by natural monopolies, e.g., public utility companies or cable television.
7. Anthony Downs, *An Economic Theory of Democracy* (New York: Harper & Row, 1957), p. 6.
8. For a forceful argument in favour of the utility-maximizing behaviour of individuals in non-economic situations, see Gary S. Becker, *The Economic Approach to Human Behaviour* (Chicago: The Univ. of Chicago Press, 1976), pp. 3-14.
9. For a lucid presentation of this assumption, see William H. Riker and Peter C. Ordeshook, *An Introduction to Positive Political Theory* (Englewood Cliffs: Prentice-Hall, 1973), pp. 12-43.
10. Success for a policy is defined for the purpose of this paper as the difference between the total support and the total opposition. This is equivalent to the notion of profit in economics.
11. R. L. Curry, Jr. and L. L. Wade, *A Theory of Political Exchange* (Englewood Cliffs: Prentice-Hall, 1968), p. 4.
12. There is also a third group: those who neither gain nor lose. But as per our assumption they are inconsequential in the political process.
13. For example, a car manufacturer might be producing both small and large cars. If the present mood among the buyers is to buy small cars, it will produce more of small cars. It will not abandon the large car plant even if it is running with a loss. It would rather wait for the upturn of the market when it can decide to produce more of large cars again.
14. W. A. Niskanen, *Bureaucracy and Representative Government* (Chicago: Aldine, 1971), p. 25.
15. For empirical justification of the assumption, see T.C. Bergstrom and R.P. Goodman, "Private Demand for Public Goods", *American Economic Review,* 63, June 1973, pp. 286-296; T. E. Borcherding and R.T. Deacon, "The Demand for Services of Non-Federal Governments", *American Economic Review*, 62, December 1972, pp. 891-901; and Robert P. Inman, "Testing Political Economy's 'as if' Proposition: Is the Median Income Voter Really Decisive?", *Public Choice,* 33(4), 1978, pp. 45-65. The median voter model hypothesizes (i) a single

public service for which, (ii) consumer-voters have single peaked preferences and (iii) voters are 'sincere' voters and can be ordered along a continuum from low to high demanders of the public service. While it is questionable whether any or all of these hypotheses conform to reality and hence, whether it really leads to an equilibrium outcome, we believe that it is a reasonable assumption for the sake of making an *estimate* of the market demand for a policy at a particular point of time.

16. Note the difference between the demand curve faced by the incumbent party in this case and if it were a purely competitive situation. In the latter case it would have been horizontal.
17. Unlike a firm in the economic market, the incumbent party does not invest a capital of its own. It simply passes on the expenses to the individuals. Therefore, the actual costs of a policy, in monetary terms, are incurred by the individuals and not by the incumbent party. The implication of this cost for the incumbent party will be discussed in the next section.
18. For an illustration of the use of this assumption in a different context, see Sam, Peltzman, "Towards a More General Theory of Regulation", *Journal of Law and Economics,* 19 (2), August 1976, pp. 211-240.

THREE

A CROSS-NATIONAL EMPIRICAL ANALYSIS

IN the previous chapter I developed three conditions for changes in policy in a democratic political system. As I had noted, in the absence of survey data only two of these are testable. They are: (i) that a marginal change in the voting support of the incumbent party will be positively related to change in a public policy; and (ii) that the turnover of the incumbent party at the election will be positively related to the changes in a public policy. In this chapter I intend to test for these two conditions using the aggregate data from the contemporary democratic regimes[1] during the period 1952–1980. Before doing so, however, it is necessary to take account of several other factors which might also affect policy change.

In the economic market, a good is not produced simply because there is a demand for the good or a firm is willing to produce it. Other environmental factors have to be conducive to such production; for example, sufficient raw material should be available, technical know-how to produce the good should exist, the industrial machinery should be available, enough labour-force should be available, etc. The nature of these environmental factors will depend on the type of good to be produced. Similarly, in a political market, the production of a policy will not depend only on the factors described by the above conditions (let me call them 'political exchange' variables), but also on several other environmental factors. In order to assess the impact of the exchange variables on the changes of a policy, I have to hold constant all other environmental factors that might also influence such changes. In the literature of the empirical policy analysis, sets of socio-economic and political variables are traditionally thought to be two competing explanations of policy changes. The socio-economic and the political variables to be included and held constant in the model will depend on the nature of policy changes we wish to explain, i.e. , the substance of our dependent variables.

The Dependent Variables

I hypothesize that the exchange variables will be positively related to changes in any public policy. However, for convenience, I chose as dependent variables only two areas of policy. This would facilitate comparison across nations and will allow for easy measurement of policy changes. The first area is the redistributive performance of the political system. A basic question that every incumbent party faces is: how large should the redistributive activity of the political system be? Or, in other words, what proportion of the total governmental expenditure should be spent in redistributive activity? One way of observing this proportion is to calculate the share of each kind of welfare expenditure in the total governmental expenditures. However, in a cross-national comparison, it is difficult to estimate changes in each aspect of welfare expenditure. In one country there may be a substantial expenditure in one aspect of welfare expenditure, say veteran benefits, because of the country's large size of military personnel; but in another country such expenditure may be absolutely nil.

Therefore, I look at the welfare expenditure in a more general way: the per cent of the total governmental expenditure transferred directly to the households (henceforth, I will refer to this only as 'transfers'). Such transfers usually include social security payments, pension payments, unemployment benefits, sickness benefits, veteran benefits, etc.[2]

A second area of public policy that I wish to use as a dependent variable is the extractive performance of the political system. The most common form of extraction is taxation. Indeed, any modern government gets most of its revenue from this source. However, it is the changes in the direct taxes which have the most visible impact on the individuals' attitude towards the government. Also, often the incumbent party uses the policy of direct taxes as an instrument for maintaining its support base. Therefore, I consider, as the second dependent variable, the per cent of the total governmental revenue coming from direct taxes.[3] Looked at from another angle, this policy, like transfer, is also utilized by the governments in their effort to redistribute the wealth in society. Therefore, both of our dependent variables may be regarded as 'redistributive' in nature.

The changes in the transfers or the direct taxes are measured by the following formula:[4]

$$C = \left| \frac{\left(\sum_{y=1}^{n} T_y/n\right) - \left(\sum_{y=1}^{m} T_y/m\right)}{\left(\sum_{y=1}^{m} T_y/m\right)} . 100 \right|$$

C: changes in transfers or direct taxes;
T: annual transfers as a percentage of the total expenditure of the national government, or, annual direct taxes as a percentage of the total revenue of the national government, for the year Y;
n: the number of years in the current observation;
m: the number of years in the previous observation.

In this measurement of changes, percentage changes rather than the first order differences are used in order to make them comparable across nations and to avoid artificially deflating the magnitude of change in nations with a relatively low value in the initial time period.

In this data, the time period between two elections in one country is taken as one observation[5]. There are 126 observations for changes in transfers and 123 observations for changes in direct taxes.[6] There are significant variations in the rates of change in transfers or direct taxes among our observations. The rate of change in transfers varies from 0.33 per cent to 25.30 per cent with a mean of 8.96. The rate of change in direct taxes varies from 0.07 per cent to 19.62 per cent with a mean of 7.18.[7] I now turn to the reasons of such variation in the policy change.

Political Exchange Variables and Policy Changes

The importance of the political exchange in public policy making has been elaborated in the earlier chapter. Here I wish to explain the measurement of two variables which are the components of political exchange: the change in the size of the incumbent coalition and the incumbency turnover. The change in the size of the incumbent coalition is measured by the absolute difference between the electoral voting support of the incumbent party in one time period and that of the previous time period.[8] Here the change in the incumbent coalition size is actually an estimate of the changes in the support groups between two time periods. I believe that this is a better estimate than measuring changes in the legislative strength of the incumbent party. Since the incumbent party's motive is to win re-election, it tries to provide benefits to its supporters in the electorate. The actual impact of the benefits or costs of a policy is felt by the electorate. The consequences of a policy for a legislator is only incidental.

The incumbency turnover is defined as the change in the party occupying the actual executive authority, the Presidency or the Prime Ministership depending on the constitutional system. Thus I have assumed that continuity in the executive authority is maintained if there are simply some changes in persons, but not in the party, occupying the executive authority.[9] The rationale of such an argument is that there is relative continuity in policies when the same party continues to occupy the executive authority. While the changes in the size of the incumbent coalition measures the quantitative change in the composition of a coalition, the turnover variable takes care of the qualitative change, if any.[10]

Socio-Economic Factors and Policy Changes

As I have pointed out in the first chapter, availability of the economic resources is an important determinant of policy change. Since the dependent variables are concerned with aspects of governmental revenue and expenditure, I hypothesize that the socio-economic environment will have significant impact on the changes in those policies. Particularly, those variables that measure changes in the socio-economic environment between two periods of time would have important influence on the changes in transfer or changes in direct taxes. I have included three such variables in the model: the rate of economic growth, the rate of population growth and the rate of inflation. In addition, a variable called openness of economy is included to take into account the impact of the international economic situation on the policy changes inside the country.

Economic growth[11] provides the resources for the extension of public expenditure and the basis for the collection of more or less revenue. In the industrializing countries where the economy expands rapidly, the redistributive activity may experience great fluctuation, either increase or decrease depending on other circumstances. If the population has already become affluent in general, but the country continues to have a high growth rate, the distributive expenditure may decline sharply. But it may also increase because of several reasons. "In an expanding economy, an elite can make economic concessions in *relative* terms without necessarily suffering any loss in *absolute* terms. In fact, if the concessions are not too large, and the rate of economy's growth is great enough, relative losses can even be accompanied by *substantial* absolute gains."[12] Rapid growth also affects other demographic characteristics which, in turn, affect the redistributive policies. For instance, Wilensky argues that affluence produces a decline in birth rates resulting in a large population of old people – at once a population in need and a political force for further social security development.[13] Also, technological changes which are often associated with rapid growth may increase unemployment levels. Thus the industrializing countries face a dilemma where "some lose part of their incomes (due to inflation) and others, because of the new problem of unemployment, lose all of their incomes".[14] In either case one would expect great changes in the redistributive policy between two time periods.

There are several reasons for expecting that rapid population growth[15] may lead to more changes in the redistributive policies. This variable serves in part as an indicator of a constraint on the political efforts to redistribute material goods.[16] More population implies that there are more people who seek redistributive material goods, which would result in more positive changes if the economy is also improving. But if the economy is stagnant, then rapid economic growth may result in large negative changes because the government utilizes the existing economic resources to satisfy other pressing needs of the growing population like school, housing, etc. Secondly, the impact of population growth is very important in the so called 'dual' economies, consisting of both the traditional agricultural sector and the smaller but more modern industrial sector. If there is rapid population growth in such a situation, it typically increases the proportion of population in the rural sector which is already over-populated and where the marginal product of labour has fallen to zero. But the numeric strength of the rural population gives it a bargaining power in democratic countries and hence the relative size of distributive expenditure increases. Thirdly, population growth rates may service as indirect indicators of other cultural conditions. Most of the countries with high fertility rates are thosc which have traditional social values but which are striving hard to be modern. The modernizing experiences are also associated with egalitarian objectives of redistributing the nation's wealth. Thus by including the population growth rate as an independent variable we are able to control for at least one other qualitative dimension, i.e., modernizing experience, by quantitative means.

I hypothesize that a high rate of inflation[17] may lead to fewer changes in distributive policy. It is often assumed that high rates of growth lead to high rates of inflation. Therefore, it is further assumed, the influence of inflation on the distributive policy occurs through its association with the rates of growth. However, my data do not support such contention. The two variables, the rate of growth and the rate of inflation, are negatively correlated (r=–.27).[18] The magnitude of this relation is fairly modest, leaving open the possibility that the rates of inflation may exert an impact independent of the rate of growth. A high rate of inflation erodes benefits making beneficiaries living on fixed incomes great sufferers. In most of such cases, the best thing that a government can do is to tie the benefits to cost-of-living escalators or to periodically increase benefits. In neither case would the proportion of transfer to the households out of the total expenditures of the government change dramatically. Furthermore, governments cannot substantially decrease benefits in an inflationary period, because the beneficiary groups are often the politically significant groups in a democratic system. Since the inflationtary pressure is felt by every group in the society, governments avoid increasing their share of the direct taxes. Therefore, I would expect the rate of inflation to be negatively related to the changes in the redistributive policy.

Cameron finds that the openness of economy[19] is the strongest predictor of the expansion of the public economy.[20] The countries which have relatively open economies are usually small in size.[21] Because of the size of these countries the governments cannot shelter their economies from the competitive risks of the international economy by any protectionist policy instrument. They rather tend to provide a variety of income supplements in the form of social security schemes, health insurance, unemployment benefits, job training, etc. The country's dependence on the vagaries of international economy would result in frequent fluctuations in the beneficiaries from such distributive policies. Since the expansion of public economy also implies the expansion of a 'tax state', the countries with open economies will have more fluctuations in tax policies as well. Thus I would expect the openness of the economy to be positively associated with my dependent variables.

The Policital Engironment and the Policy Changes

Another competing paradigm to explain the changes in a policy is what is known as the 'political environments matter' hypothesis. In this study it has been explicitly assumed that politics – especially electoral politics – exerts a significant influence on the public policies. Besides this type of politics at an operational level, several scholars regard the political environmental conditions as important determinants of policy, as I have discussed in the first chapter. In order to explore the influence of the political environment on the dependent variables, I will examine four such variables: the ideology of the incumbent party; the frequency of the executive facing the electorate; the effectiveness of the executive in the legislature (existence of the minority governments); and the constitutional design of the distribution of power between the different levels of government.

In the arguments that posit a relationship between political factors and policy outcomes, the role of ideology is sometimes regarded as important. However, there is considerable debate in policy analysis about its actual impact. Wilensky finds that ideology does not explain national differences in social security spending.[22] Similarly Jackman finds that the strength of the socialist parties has no impact on the distribution of material goods.[23] There is also contrary evidence which suggests that ideology may be relevant in the process of policy making. For example, Castle concludes that "partisan control of the government is a major determinant of policy outputs".[24] Davis, Dempster and Wildavsky contend that the magnitude of the increments granted to American federal agencies is influenced by such partisan variables as the strength of the liberal wing of the Democrats in the Congress and Democratic control of the Presidency.[25] Keeping in mind such contradictory evidence, I have included the ideology of the incumbent party[26] in this model for exploratory purpose only. Since our dependent variables measure absolute changes in policy I do not expect that there will be a great deal of the impact of ideology. However, with a dependent variable which measures relative changes, ideology might have a significant impact on policy making. In that case, ideology may indeed be a part of the political exchange process as a measure of change in the nature of supporters. In a way, the incumbency turnover variable is also a measure of an ideological change, since in most cases of turnover the power changes hands from left-oriented parties to right-oriented parties and vice versa.

Several empirical studies about the public expenditure in the American states have been less concerned about the ideological position of the government than with the extent of political competition. Ever since Key[27] stressed the importance of the two party competition of bifactionalism in one party states as a determinant of policies favouring the 'have-nots' in society, there has been a vast literature both supporting and opposing his argument. There are some[28] whose findings indicate that party competition has substantial impact on the welfare expenditure. There are others[29] who have argued that after controlling for various measures of economic development, the apparent connection between the party competition and the welfare expenditure disappears. However, in all these studies of either side of the argument there is an implicit assumption that the voters tend to reward the incumbents who can increase their income in some way, even if it is by sheer economic development. Empirical studies[30] also support this assertion. Hence, the incumbents attempt to use the spending policies to enhance their support in anticipation of elections.[31] This would result in a 'political business cycle'[32] with uunusually increased spending immediately before and after the election. Thus the frequency of elections is an important determinant in the governmental expenditures or the tax policies. I expect, following the above literature, that they will be positively associated.[33]

In almost every country both the executive and the legislature share the responsibilities of policy making. Often the executive initiates the policies and the legislature approve them.[34] Although as the initiator, the executive branch has a major voice in the future shape of policies, it has to secure enough support in the legislature for its final approval. Thus the effectiveness of the incumbent party's policy is dependent on its relationship with the legislature. While in most cases the incumbent party has a majority support in the legislature, in some countries a sizable number of administrations have to manage with only a minority support.[35] A minority government not only implies absence of executive control but also different situations in legislative-executive relations[36] leading to frequent bargaining and policy maneuvering. All these impede the policy making initiative of the incumbent party. Therefore, Powell predicts that minority governments, which are dependent on the outside support of other parties in the legislature, should be restrained in their manipulation of the economy.[37] If one follows this argument, one would expect non-positive relationship between the minority governments and the policy changes.[38] However, one has to keep in mind that the minority governments in my data are only a special subset of all minority governments, i.e., those which have survived at least for two years. It excludes, therefore, the "caretaker" governments which remain passive in policy formation. Whether there will be more or less policy change in these cases will be very much dependent on the sources of their legislative support, i.e., the nature outside supporters and the type of bargains they make.

The privilege of formulating policies is not only shared horizontally, with the legislature, but also vertically, with other governments at the state and the local levels. In cases where no single level of authority decides about the total governmental revenue or expenditure for the country and where the institutional structure guarantees that one level of the government can spend funds raised by other levels, the revenue or expenditure of a single level of government will be affected by the action of other levels. Hence, the greater the number of the levels of government, the greater will be the fluctuation in a single level of government. On the basis of the number of different levels of government, one can divide the countries into the federal and the unitary ones. In spite of Riker's assertion that the constitutional and administrative arrangements are "accidents of federalism", he nonetheless concedes that they "deeply affect the style of public policy making", if not the outcome.[39] If, for example, the outcome for the individual is certain level of taxation and the local and the state governments have already extracting too much from them, the national government perhaps might think of reducing its own rate of taxes, or vice versa. Thus I would expect that there will be more fluctuations in policies in federal countries.[40]

To sum up, I expect all independent variables, except the rate of inflation and the minority support in the legislature, to be positively associated with the dependent variables. I expect the association of the rate of inflation to be negative and that of the minority support in the legislature to be either negative or zero.

Findings and Discussion

Tables 3.1 and 3.2 present the results of multiple regression analyses of three possible explanations (political exchange variables, socio-economic situation and political environment) of the changes in the direct transfer to the households and the changes in the direct taxes respectively. Those analyses support the following conclusions:

Changes in the size of the incumbent coalition lead to changes in transfer and direct taxes (B = .16 and .21 respectively).[41] Since the incumbent party tries to provide for its own supporters more benefits and less costs from a policy, any changes in its support base are reflected in the changes in policies as well. Compared to the impact of a simple change in the number of beneficiaries, we find that there is greater impact of the changes in the composition of beneficiaries. The turnover of the incumbent party at the election has a positive association with the policy changes (B = .28 and .36). As the regression coefficients of both of these variables are positive and t-values are quite high, the data support the contention that the political exchange mechanism does play a role in the policy making process. However, the limited magnitude of the variations explained

TABLE 3.1: Changes in Transfers

Multiple Regression Analysis of the Impact of the Political Exchange, Socio-economic and Political Variables on the Changes in the Direct Transfers to the Households.

	All Variables		Political Exchange Variables		Socio-Economic Variables		Political Environment Variables	
	Regression Coefficients	Standardized Regression Coef.	Regression Coefficients	Standardized Regression Coef.	Regression Coefficients	Standardized Regression Coef.	Regression Coefficients	Standardized Regression Coef.
	1	2	3	4	5	6	7	8
Change in Size of Incumbent Coalition	0.15 (2.13)*	.16	0.17 (2.22)	.18				
Incumbency Turnover	2.11 (3.65)	.28	2.61 (4.11)	.34				
The Rate of Economic Growth	1.06 (3.66)	.30			0.86 (2.75)	.24		
The Rate of Population Growth	1.22 (1.85)	.15			1.70 (2.44)	.21		
The Rate of Inflation	0.14 (1.47)	.11			0.15 (1.50)	.13		
Openness of Economy	0.07 (3.06)	.25			0.11 (4.49)	.39		
Ideology of the Incumbents	–0.62 (1.08)	–.08					–0.71 (1.07)	–.09
Frequency of Elections	–8.01 (1.97)	–.18					–11.69 (2.83)	–.26

(Contd.)

TABLE 3.1 – *Contd.*

	1	2	3	4	5	6	7	8
Minority Support in Legislature	4.89 (4.43)	.32					5.53 (4.27)	.36
Federal Structure of Government	0.40 (0.33)	.03					–0.15 (0.13)	–.01
Intercept	–2.96		3.21		–3.32		14.16	
N=126	K=10 R-square: .47		K=2 R-square: .17		K=4 R-square: .20		K=4 R-square: .22	

* t-value in the parentheses

TABLE 3.2: Changes in Direct Taxes

Multiple Regression Analysis of the Impact of the Political Exchange, Socio-economic and Political Variables on the Changes in the Direct Taxes.

	All Variables		Political Exchange Variables		Socio-Economic Variables		Political Environment Variables	
	Regression Coefficients	Standardized Regression Coef.	Regression Coefficients	Standardized Regression Coef.	Regression Coefficients	Standardized Regression Coef.	Regression Coefficients	Standardized Regression Coef.
	1	2	3	4	5	6	7	8
Change in Size of Incumbent Coalition	0.16 (2.60)*	.21	0.15 (2.40)	.20				
Incumbency Turnover	1.64 (3.18)	.26	2.58 (4.99)	.41				

(Contd.)

TABLE 3.2 – *Contd.*

	1	2	3	4	5	6	7	8
The Rate of Economic Growth	–0.53 (2.07)	–.18			–0.81 (3.03)	–.28		
The Rate of Population Growth	1.41 (2.39)	.20			2.23 (3.73)	.32		
The Rate of Inflation	0.01 (0.06)	.01			–0.04 (0.43)	–.04		
Openness of Economy	0.04 (2.08)	.18			0.05 (2.49)	.22		
Ideology of the Incumbents	–0.54 (1.07)	–.09					–0.68 (1.22)	–.11
Frequency of Elections	–7.97 (2.22)	–.21					–17.06 (4.89)	–.45
Minority Support in Legislature	2.02 (2.06)	.16					1.94 (1.76)	.15
Federal Structure of Government	2.31 (2.15)	.20					2.78 (2.81)	.24
Intercept	4.82		1.42		5.66		14.39	
N=123	K=10 R-square: .42		K=2 R-square: .23		K=4 R-square: .18		K=4 R-square: .21	

* t-value in the parentheses

by these two variables (17% and 23%) indicates that several other factors do play a major role in explaining the policy changes.

The rate of economic growth provides contradictory results. While in the case of transfer the regression coefficient is positive (B = .30) as per our expectation, in the case of direct taxes it is negative (B = –.18). In neither case can the null hypothesis of no effect be accepted at .05 significance level. The relatively strong positive association in the case of transfers indicates that there are more changes in countries experiencing rapid economic growth. Perhaps the reason the coefficient is negative in the case of the direct taxes is that there is no pressing necessity to increase taxes when there is high rate of growth. If there is any necessity for additional expenditure in such cases, like that of Japan, larger revenues can be obtained by simply applying a constant public share to a larger economic product. But in cases of very modest growth rates, like that of U.K., taxes have to be increased to meet the demands for additional public goods. Thus I find, in general, that economic growth rate is significantly related to the changes of transfer or of direct taxes. However, the opposite direction of the coefficients in both the variables is rather puzzling and needs further investigation.

The rate of population growth is positively and significantly related to the depenedent variables (B = .15 and .20). Apparently, a large increase in population, like that of India, require more transfer payments which also means extracting more taxes. Or, a modest increase in population, like that of Finland, may result in only a modest change in-redistributive policies.

Contrary to my expectation, the rate of inflation contributes positively to the changes in transfers and direct taxes (B= .11 and .01). But the impact is quite modest and with their low t-values I can accept the null hypothesis that there is no impact at all. Perhaps the reason for such limited effects is that the rate of inflation is almost uniform across the countries. The pattern everywhere is similar: low rate of inflation in the fifties, moderate in the sixties and very high in the seventies. Moreover, a high rate of inflation is generally associated with a general expansion of the expenditure and revenue of the government including the transfers and the direct taxes, but without any significant changes in the *proportion* of the transfers or direct taxes in the total budget.

Governments of countries with open economies are more likely to experience changes in their transfers and direct tax policies than those with relatively closed economies (B = .25 and .18). High dependence on the international market has its impact on the fluctuations of domestic redistributive policies. Perhaps such dependence combined with the smallness of size of these countries result in a pattern of economic growth that has great deal of impact on the redistributive policies.

Like the political exchange variables, all the four socio-economic variables together explain only a modest amount of variation (20% and 18%) in the dependent variables. This implies that although the economic variables do matter, they are not the only predictors of redistributive policy changes, as one group of scholarly literature indicates.

The left oriented governments do not bring about a lot of changes in redistributive policies (B = –.08 and –.09). The low t-values indicate that I can even accept, at .05 significance level, the null hypothesis that these parameter estimates are zero. It is perhaps because we are examining absolute changes in policies. Even if a left oriented government increased the expenditures on transfer, its magnitude is probably modest compared to the extent of decreases in such expenditures by right oriented governments. Or, it may be that the left oriented governments expand the overall expenditures and revenues of the government, as they are sometimes expected to do, but changes in the *proportion* of the transfers or direct taxes in the budget remained relatively modest. It is also probable that the major effect of ideology is through incumbency turnover which partly reflects the ideological changes. In any case, our analysis does not claim to resolve the issue as to whether the ideological position of the government has any impact on the policy changes.

Contrary to what the existing scholarly literatures tend to establish, the frequency of elections dampen the extent of changes in public policies (B = –.18 and –.21). It is apparent that any tendency to provide more benefits during the election years is more than offset by other effects. Since no government likes to increase taxes in election years, more elections would imply less changes in direct taxes. Another reason for such a negative effect might be that I did not measure the changes in policy of each year to capture the effect of an election year on the changes in policy. I am looking at changes over a longer period, between two elections, implying thereby that most of the extraordinary changes in the election years have been averaged out in the expenditure or revenue of the total period. However, a more plausible hypothesis is that in the countries with frequent elections, the incumbent party is usually afraid, from a strategic point of view, to try to experiment with any drastic policy changes. On the other hand, in the countries which have a longer time between two elections, the incumbent party can afford to make such experiments and, if the cost of such changes are too high, can conveniently back out before the next election approaches.

Contrary to my expectation, existence of a minority support in the legislature positively and significantly affects the changes in the transfer and direct taxes (B = .32 and .16). Presumably, the legislators providing the outside support to the incumbent party prevail on it to bring about significant changes, or the incumbent party feels obliged to cater to the whims of various groups in the legislature in order to continue in power. These arguments are plausible because in my data I have excluded the observations whose time period is less than two years. Quite probably, minority governments that have been afraid to manipulate the economy freely because of the lack of majority have either resigned or been outvoted in the legislature within that time. Those who have survived beyond two years, and are included in our data, probably have managed with stable outside support, but with a very weak bargaining power of their own. In such cases, the legislators providing outside support very likely have forced the incumbent party to make drastic changes in policies beneficial to them. Thus one can argue that a *stable* minority government will change redistributive policies. There could also be another explanation that the countries with frequent minority governments have delegated the power to formulate redistributive policies to the bureaucratic mechanisms and these are responding quickly to the needs for change.[42]

The federal structure of the government tends to contribute to the changes in redistributive policies (B = .03 and .20). However, the t-value of the regression coefficient in the case of transfers is very low and the coefficient becomes negative when we isolate the political variables. Therefore, I conclude that this relationship is weak. However, the positive impact of the federal structure of government on the changes in direct taxes is perhaps because the major source of revenue of federal governments is usually from direct taxes, while both direct and indirect taxes are major sources of revenue of the unitary governments and hence, in the latter case the proportion of direct taxes in the total revenue can be relatively stable. But no such distinction exists between the federal and the unitary governments in their patterns of expenditure on the transfer to the households.[43]

TABLE 3.3: **Chnges in Transfers and Direct Taxes**

Multiple Regression Analysis of the Impact of the Political Exchange, Socio-economic and Political Variables on the Changes in the Direct Transfers to the Households and in the Direct Taxes.

	Transfers		Direct Taxes	
	Regression Coefficients	Standardized Regression Coeff.	Regression Coefficients	Standardized Regression Coeff.
Change in Size of Incumbent Coalition	0.15 (2.22)*	.16	0.17 (2.71)	.21
Incumbency Turnover	2.28 (4.03)	.29	1.64 (3.23)	.26
The Rate of Economic Growth	0.96 (3.45)	.27	–0.54 (2.20)	–.18
The Rate of Population Growth	1.27 (2.08)	.16	1.46 (2.51)	.21
Openness of Economy	0.07 (3.39)	.26	0.04 (2.02)	.18
Frequency of Elections	–5.18 (1.43)	–.11	–6.64 (2.04)	–.17
Minority Support in Legislature	4.92 (4.56)	.32	1.90 (1.96)	.15
Federal Structure of Government	—	—	2.11 (2.05)	.18
Intercept	–4.27		3.36	
	R-square: .46 N=126; K=7		R-square: .41 N=123; K=8	

* t-value in the parentheses

The four political environment variables in the model, like the political exchange and socio-economic variables, explain only a modest amount of variation (22% and 21%) in the changes in the policies considered here. Even after including all the three groups of variables in one model, except those variables which are not significant, the variances explained are only 46 per cent in the case of transfers and 41 per cent in the case of direct taxes (Table 2.3). This leaves open the question whether, if any more explanatory variables should be included in the model. As I have noted earlier, because of the lack of data I have not been able to include another exchange variable (the difference between the median voter's marginal benefit and marginal cost from a policy) which I theoretically expect to be related to the policy changes. Even without that variable one should note the fact that the political exchange variables explain as much, if not more, of variation in the model compared to the socio-economic and political variables. The R-squares of all the three groups of variables are almost equal. Therefore, I am fairly confident that the choices of the people and of the decision makers in the process of exchange in the political market are important determinants of policy making in a democratic political system.

NOTES

1. As defined in G Bingham Powell, Jr., *Contemporary Democracies: Participation, Stability and Violence* (Cambridge: Harvard Univ. Press, 1982), pp. 2-7. To identify the set of contemporary democracies, Powell looked for the political systems meeting *all* of the following criteria: (i) the legitimacy of the government rests on a claim to represent the desires of its citizens; (ii) the organized arrangement that regulates this bargain is the competitive political election; (iii) most

adults can participate in the electoral process, both as voters and as candidates for important political office; (iv) citizens' votes are secret and not coerced; (v) citizens and leaders enjoy basic freedom of speech, press, assembly and organization; and (vi) the population of the country is at least one million. Out of his list of contemporary democratic regimes, I have excluded Israel (because of war and other factors resulting in unusually sharp changes in policies), Jamaica (because of the non-availability of relevant data), Switzerland (because of the peculiarity of the decision making structures) and Turkey (because of the military takeoever). The 21 countries that I have included are: Austria, Belgium, Canada, Costa Rica, Denkark, Finland, France, West Germany, India, Ireland, Italy, Japan, Netherlands, New Zealand, Norway, Sri Lanka, Sweden, United Kingdom, United States and Venezuela. The time period between two elections in a country is taken as one observation (see footnote 6. and Appendix). Strictly speaking, my data contains nearly the universe of the countries which were continuously democratic during 1952-1980. However, this can also be considered as a sample of all democratic countries that ever existed and will exist in the world. Therefore, I have included the t-statistics for tests of significance while analysing the data.

2. The data for all countries except Denmark and the U.S.A. were obtained from United Nations, *Yearbook of National Accounts Statistics* (various volumes). The data for Denmark and the U.S.A. were obtained from Organization for Economic Cooperation and Development, *National Accounts of OECD Countries* (various volumes). Although there is some possibility of discrepency between the two sources of data, for our purposes comparability is maintained because I am looking at the *percentages of changes* in transfers only.
3. There is some controversy about the definition of the term 'direct taxes'. I have simply accepted each country's statement about the amount of 'direct taxes' collected and reported to our data sources, irrespective of how the country defines the term. Usually this a tax on income and wealth. The data for France and the U.S.A. were obtained from OECD, *ibid.* and for all other countries were obtained from UN, *ibid.*
4. To give an example of how this formula has been operationalized, let us consider the case of country 'X' which had elections

in the month of January in 1963, 1966 and 1970. The period 1963-1965 constitutes the time period in the previous observation with m number of years, or in this case three years. The period 1966-1969 is the time period in the current observation with n number of years, or in this case four years. The share of transfers in the expenditures or the share of direct taxes in the revenues is averaged for each time period. If the average annual transfer is 25 per cent of the budget during 1963-1965 and is 30 per cent during 1966-1969, then the increase is by 5 per cent, or the change 'C' for the period 1966-1969 is 20 per cent compared to the previous period. This change, 20 per cent is predicted by the independent variables.

5. The only exception is that, if between two elections, the administration changes hands and the successor belongs to a different political party I would have counted these as two observations. In these data there happens to be no such observation, given the two-year principle (see the next footnote). However, if the successor is of the same party, I have counted it as one observation. For example, in the U.S.A., Nixon was re-elected as the President in 1972 and Ford succeeded him in 1974. But I have regarded the entire period of 1973-1976 as one observation, a Republican Presidency.
6. Several observations have been excluded because of one or both of the following reasons: (i) if the data for the relevant time period are not available; and (ii) if the incumbent party/parties are in power for less than two years. The justification of the second exclusion principle is that the incumbent party needs at least two years to implement its own policies effectively. The French and the Venezuelan observations have been included since 1965 and 1963 elections respectively. The periods of 1958-1964 in the case of France and of 1958-1962 in the case of Venezuela were utilized as the base periods for the purpose of estimating the changes in policy in the subsequent periods. The break up of the number of observations for the 21 countries is the following: Australia: 9; Austria: 7; Belgium: 8; Canada: 7; Costa Rica: 3; Denmark: 5; Finland: 6; France: 3; W. Germany: 7; India: 4; Ireland: 7; Italy: 6; Japan: 8; Netherlands: 5; New Zealand: 7; Norway: 7; Sri Lanka: 4; Sweden: 7; U.K. : 6; U.S.A.: 7; Venezuela: 3. In the case of the direct taxes, three observations, one each in Belgium, Canada and Ireland are ex-

cluded because of the non-availability of data.

7. Note that there is no observation where the rate of change is zero. This implies that there is no case where a policy is in equilibrium, which one should normally expect in the real world.
8. Among the observations, this measure varied from 0 to 41.0. The basic data on the electoral support for political parties were collected from Thomas Mackie and Richard Rose, *The International Almanac of Electoral History,* 2nd. Ed. (New York: Free Press, 1982). Wherever necessary, additional informations were collected from *Keesing's Archives* and various country studies. The informations about the incumbency of parties were collected from the *Political Handbook of the World* (various volumes).
9. For example, in Venezuela, Betancourt was elected as the President in 1958 and Leoni in the next election in 1963. But I did not count that as a turnover because both belong to the same party, i.e., Accion Democratica.
10. The incumbency turnover is coded as: 1=no turnover; 2= partial turnover (in the case of a coalition of several parties occupying the executive authority, if some of them lose incumbency or if some parties who were in the opposition enter into the incumbent coalition); 3=total turnover. Among our 126 observations there are 64 no turnovers, 27 partial turnovers and 35 total turnovers.
11. This variable is measured as the average annual rate of growth of G.D.P. at constant prices during the decade in which the observation occurs. The data have been compiled from the United Nations, *Statistical Yearbook* (various volumes).
12. Gerhard Lenski, *Power and Privilege: A Theory of Social Stratification* (New York: McGraw-Hill, 1966), p. 314 (Italics in the original)
13. Harold L. Wilensky, *The 'New Corporatism', Centralization and the Welfare State* (Beverly Hills: Sage, 1976), p. 13.
14. Mancur Olson, Jr., "Rapid Growth as a destabilizing Force", *Journal of Economic History,* 23 (December, 1963), p. 536.
15. It is measured as the average annual rate of growth of the population during the decade in which the observation occurs. The data have been compiled from the United Nations, *Statistical Yearbook* (various volumes).
16. See, for example, Robert W. Jackman, *Politics and Social*

Equality: A Comparative Analysis (New York: John Wiley, 1975), p. 48.

17. It is measured as the average annual rate of inflation during the decade in which the observation occurs. The data have been compiled from the United Nations, *Statistical Yearbook* (various volumes)
18. See, Appendix B.
19. This variable is operationalized as the total of imports and exports as a per centage of the gross national product (IMEX). In my data I have measured this variable as the average annual level of IMEX during the decade in which the observation occurs. The data have been compiled from the United Nations, *Statistical Yearbook* (various volumes).
20. David R. Cameron, "The Expansion of the Public Economy: A Comparative Analysis", *American Political Science Review,* 72(4), December, 1978.
21. The examples of some of the countries in which IMEX levels are very high are: Belgium, Ireland, Netherland and Norway.
22. Harold L. Wilensky, *The Welfare State and Equality: Structural and Ideological Roots of Public Expenditure* (Berkeley: Univ. of California Press, 1975) p.45
23. Robert W. Jackman, *Politics and Social Equality: A Comparative Analysis* (New York: John Wiley, 1975), p. 134.
24. Francis G. Castles, "The Impact of Parties on Public Expenditure" in his edited, *The Impact of Parties: Politics and Policies in Democratic Capitalist States* (Beverly Hills: Sage, 1982), p.88.
25. Otto A. Davis, M.A.H. Dempster and Aaron Wildavsky, "Towards a Predictive Theory of Budgetary Process", *British Journal of Political Science,* 4, 1974.
26. My coding of the ideology of the incumbent party is very simple: 1= right oriented party; 2= a coalition of right and left oriented parties; and 3= left oriented party. While judging whether a party is right oriented or left oriented I have relied on the position of the party compared to the other parties *in* the country but *not across* the countries because I believe that, when a party changes a policy, it wants to show the electorate its position compared to the other party/parties in the country, not simply to convince the electorate of its own ideological position. Thus, for example, I have regarded both the

Democratic Party in the U.S.A. and the Labour Party in the U.K. as left oriented, although the former may not be as 'leftist' as the latter. My judgement about the ideology of a party in each country is based on the eividence found in Alan J. Day and Henry W. Degenhardt, *Political Parties in the World* (Essex: Longman, 1980).

27. V.O. Key, Jr., *Southern Politics* (New York: Vintage Books, 1949).
28. See, for example, Charles F. Cnudde and Donald J. McCrone, "Party Competition and Welfare Policies in American States", *American Political Science Review,* 63, 1969; I. Sharkansky and R. Hofferbert, "Dimensions of State Politics, Economics and Public Policy", *ibid.*, 63, 1969; and Edward T. Jennings, Jr., "Competition, Constituencies and Welfare Policies in American States", *ibid.*, 73, 1979.
29. See, for example, Richard E. Dawson and James A. Robinson, "Inter-Party Competition, Economic Variables and Welfare Policies in the American States". *Journal of Politics,* 25, 1963; Thomas R. Dye, *Politics, Economics and the Public* (Chicago: Rand McNally, 1966); and Richard Winter, "Party Control and Policy Change", *American Journal of Political Science,* 20, 1976.
30. Gerald H. Kramer, "Short-term Fluctuations in U.S. Voting Behaviour, 1896-1964", *American Political Science Review,* 65, 1971; and Edward Tufte, "Determinants of the Outcome of Midterm Congressional Elections", *ibid.*, 69, 1975.
31. This has been demonstrated by Edward Tufte, *Political Control of the Economy* (Princeton: Princeton Univ. Press, 1978).
32. William D. Nordhaus, "The Political Business Cycle", *Review of Economic Studies,* 42, 1975.

33. In my data each country gets a score of the frequency of elections by computing the annual average of the number of elections a country faced during 1953-1977 (1958-1977 for France and Venezeuela). The basic data about elections have been collected from Charles Lewis Taylor and David A. Jodice, *World Handbook of Political and Social Indicators,* 3rd Ed., Vol. II (New Haven: Yale Univ. Press, 1983), pp. 80-84. While counting the number of elections I have included all elections in which the incumbent party faced an act of collective choice,

whether or not it is for its own election to the national executive which demarcates the time periods in my data. Three types of elections of national importance are coded: popular elections to the national legislature, popular elections to the national chief executives and the national referenda. No exclusions were made on the basis of suffrage limitations, competitiveness, legality or the significance of the election in the country's political process. Excluded are the elections held within the national legislature or party congresses, popular elections to trade union or political party leadership and local elections. Totals have been calculated to exclude double counting when elections for chief executive and legislature were held the same day. The rationale of including all popular elections in the data is that I would expect to find a reflection of all elections on the incumbent party's policies, as is evident from several studies on the mid-term Congressional elections in the U.S.A. See, for example, Tufte, "Determinants", *op cit.*

34. Traditionally, the primary function of the legislature is supposed to be legislation (policy making?). Lately, there has been so much erosion in this function and so much of intrusion by the executive in this sphere that two scholars on legislatures have preferred the term 'conflict management' function instead of 'law making'. See, Gerhard Loewenberg and Samuel C. Patterson, *Comparing Legislatures* (Boston: Little, Brown, 1979). Also see the chapter on "Decline of Legislatures" in K.C. Wheare, *Legislatures* (London:Oxford Univ. Press, 1963).
35. By one count, in the twelve western democracies which have experienced minority and/or supported minority governments from the formation of the first post-war administration following free elections to the July 1, 1971, 35.8% of the total administrations had minority support in the legislature. See, Valentine Herman and John Pope, "Minority Governments in Western Democracies", *British Journal of Political Science, 3, 1973, p. 194.*
36. See, G. Bingham Powell, Jr., *Contemporary Democracies: Participation, Stability and Violence* (Cambridge: Harvard Univ. Press, 1982), pp. 142-144.
37. *Ibid.*, p. 209
38. Minority support in the legislature has been coded as: (i) 1= if the incumbent party has less than 50% support in the legisla-

ture; (ii) 0= otherwise. Out of our 126 observations 31 are minority governments. In counting the support in the legislature, U.S.A. is the most difficult case because of its frequent non-partisan voting in the Congress. Since almost all the Presidents get approval of the Congress for most of their policies, I have coded all U.S.A. observations as 0.

39. William H. Riker, "Federalism", in Fred I. Greenstein and Nelson W. Polsby (eds), *Handbook of Political Science*, Vol. 5 (Reading: Addison-Wesley, 1975), p. 144 (italics mine).

40. The federal structure variable is coded as: (i) 1=federal; and (ii) 0= otherwise. Observations from the following countries are coded as federal: Australia, Austria, Canada, West Germany, India, U.S.A. and Venezuela.

41. Here and in the subsequent paragraphs 'B'represents the standardized regression coefficient.

42. In my model I have used the minority government as an intercept dummy. I also tried to use it as a slope dummy: turnover multiplied by the minority government. I found that in cases of the minority governments with a turnover the coefficient tends to decline in case of the transfers and tends to rise in case of the direct taxes. However, in neither cases the coefficients of the slope dummy variable are statistically significant.

43. In this case also I tried to use the federal structure of government as a slope dummy: turnover multiplied by the federal government. I found that in federal countries with turnover the coefficient tends to rise a little in the case of both the dependent variables. But in neither case the coefficient of the slope dummy variable is statistically significant.

FOUR

CONCLUSION

I started this study by asking the question: why do the policy makers formulate a redistributive policy in the way they do? Some scholars have tried to answer this question by saying that the data should speak for themselves and following a pure correlational or regressional analysis. Some others have tried to provide theoretical explanations without providing any empirical evidences which support such explanations. More appropriately, however, any explanation of the determinants of a policy should be theoretically plausible and should also be supported by data. If a theory is not supported by data, it needs to be modified. As Hempel explains:[1]

> The formulation of a theory will require the specification of two kinds of principles; let us call them internal principles and bridge principles for short. The former will characterize the basic entities and processes invoked by the theory and the laws to which they are assumed to conform. The latter will indicate how the processes envisaged by the theory are related to empirical phenomena with which we are acquainted, and which the theory may then explain, predict or retrodict.

This study is an attempt to use both the 'internal principles' and the 'bridge principles' while explaining the policy decisions. I have tried first to explain policy choices by means of the principles of political exchange (the internal principles) and then to test the explanations with bridge principles based on my data set.

My predecessors in this kind of investigation have tried to answer the above question in three different ways: with the 'political environment matters' hypothesis, with the economic resources model and with the rational choice approach. I pointed out in the first chapter that some of the deficiencies in these approaches can be avoided by regarding the policies as the outcome of a political exchange process between the policy makers and the policy takers. Policy makers use the policies as instruments for providing benefits to their future supporters. In the second chapter, I characterized the structure of the market for political exchange as monopolistic competition. The assumptions about the behaviour of policy makers, policy takers and the nature of the political market led to three conditions of change in the policy output: the difference between the median voter's marginal benefit and marginal cost, the marginal change in the size of the beneficiaries and the extent of turnover at the election. The first condition could not be tested because of the absence of the relevant data. In the third chapter, I tested the impact of the other two 'political exchange' variables and of several political and economic environmental variables on policy changes. The two dependent variables in the model are: expenditures on the direct transfers to households and revenue from the direct taxes.

I found that both the political exchange variables -- change in the size of the incumbent coalition and incumbency turnover -- have positive and significant influences on policy change. Among the economic variables, the rate of economic growth leads to more changes in the case of transfers, but less changes in the case of direct taxes.

Countries with rapid population growth or an open economy experience more policy changes. But the rate of inflation has very little impact and its coefficients are not significant. Among the political environment variables, a country with frequent elections has fewer policy changes while a stable minority government provides more changes. In a federal structure of government, there is more change in the direct tax policy, but there is very little impact in the case of transfers and, in the case of the latter, the coefficient is not statistically significant. The ideology of the incumbent party does not seem to have any significant impact on either of the dependent variables. On the whole, 46 per cent of variation in the changes in transfers and 41 per cent of variation in the changes in direct taxes are explained by all the independent variables whose coefficients are statistically significant. When I tested the impact of the variables representing the political exchange, socio-economic structures and political environments separately on these two dependent variables, each group of variables explain approximately one-fifth of the variation in the policy changes.

These statistical tests confirm my contention that political exchange plays an important part as a determinant of policy outcomes and that the policy makers do indeed provide inducements for their future supporters. I also find that political exchange as a paradigm has as much explanatory power as the paradigms of political and economic environments.

As I noted in chapter 1, the importance of the process political exchange has been recognized in empirical studies by Hibbs, Castles and others.[2] Evidences in these studies indicate that an inductive theory of political exchange can be easily developed. Or, the theory presented in this study can be suitably modified and generalized to incorporate all these accumulated evidences. There is a striking similarity of conclusions of this study with those of the above mentioned works. Although more work is needed to be done to arrive at any comprehensive 'knowledge' derived from these studies, it is not premature to argue that self interest of the political actors is the main driving force in the policy making process. Also, as Bunce and Pryor[3] suggest, the policy making process is almost similar in both democratic and non-democratic countries. If that is true, then I would suspect that the process of political exchange may be in operation in non-democratic countries as well. Of course, in these countries the institutions which define the structure of the political market would be different. One may have to investigate the process of coalition building among the political elites or the nature of allocation of funds and powers to different individuals and groups instead of the nature of party system or the role of elections. However, any such generalization should await further work.

Some of the results of the analyses of this dissertation are quite puzzling. There are several variables which do not have the impact that is theoretically expected. Specifically, the rate of economic growth has opposite impact on each of the two dependent variables. One needs to further investigate whether the negative effect is something typical in taxing policies or the relationship is constrained by any other intervening variables.

Similarly, the frequency of election has negative impact, contrary to the theoretical expectation. One needs to further investigate its influence on the motivations of the policy makers. Also, frequent elections might be imposing several organizational constraints. For instance, a country with frequent elections may have several "caretaker" governments which do not take policy initiatives. Or, a government with short tenure might be too much dependent on the bureaucracy which tends to maintain the *status quo*. Similar investigations have also to be made in the case of the stable minority governments. One needs to find out the composition of these governments and whether it has any extremist parties or not. One has to also observe the composition and the nature of support of those supporting from outside.

Of the three conditions of policy change mentioned in chapter 2, the one which could not be tested for lack of data is: the difference between the median voters' marginal benefit and the marginal cost from a policy. Data might be obtained but it would be extremely expensive to gather. In order to discover the impact of this condition, one has to first identify the median voters. One can look at the survey data in each country and identify the median voters from several socio-economic background questions. Or, to simplify the process, one can simply identify the voters with the median income. Then one can ask these voters the extent of benefit they would derive and the costs they would incur from various units of a policy. If in the previous time period one notices more differences in their marginal benefits and marginal costs from the units of policy available during that time period, then one would expect more changes in that policy in the present time period. This investigation can be replicated in each of the democratic countries.

Let me caution the reader about some of the limitations of this study. First, the process of political exchange, as developed here, is not a general theory of political exchange. It only pertains to a very limited aspect of political activity: the process of policy making in anticipation of future elections. It is conceivable, however, that similar processes might have significant effects in several other aspects of political life involving both cooperation and conflict.[4] The theory needs to be further refined and generalized and tested with data both at the micro and macro level.

Second, for successful testing of such a theory, one needs to use not only aggregate data but also individual level data. Are the individual leaders mainly concerned about the preferences of the citizens when they formulate a policy? Are the choices of the citizens made after a cost-benefit calculus or are some other factors playing a role? I have not been able to answer such questions in this study. Richness of this theory can be exploited if individual level data can be utilized in verifying it.

Third, I have tested the theory with only two dependent variables. Similar tests can be replicated in other policy areas. Indeed, one way to conduct a test of the theory may be to locate all policy areas that are electorally significant in a country and to see if an optimal allocation of the resources is made by the policy makers. Although outwardly this approach seems reasonable, it could create both theoretical and empirical problems. As is well known in social choice theory, there can be no equilibrium of outcome by majority decision when choice is made between more than two alternatives.[5] If we accept this logic, then a policy maker can never know which policy has majority support, so that he will allocate more resources to it. Or, he may find that every policy has a majority support. Therefore, I have assumed in this study that a policy maker will try to maximize the probability of success of each of the electorally salient policies. However, one needs to further investigate whether this is empirically true.

Fourth, I have also assumed in this study that voting in an election is the most important action on the part of citizens in the process of political exchange. One can also investigate several other forms of political interaction which may have impact on the policy making, viz, the interaction between the policy makers and the party activists, the legislators, the bureaucrats, the journalists, etc. One has to remember that the actions of these individuals are equally important in the incumbent party's re-election effort.

Thus, the explanation of policy making as a process of political exchange needs further elaboration and refinement. Still, I have given the theory substantial support, enough indeed, to justify the further investigation that I have specified.

NOTES

1. Carl G. Hempel, *Philosophy of Natural Science* (Englewood Cliffs: Prentice-Hall, 1966), pp.72-73.
2. See, footnote No. 46 of Chapter 1.
3. Valerie Bunce, *Do New Leaders Make a Difference? Executive Succession and Public Policy Under Capitalism and Socialism* (Princeton: Princeton Univ. Press, 1981); Frederick Pryor, *Public Expenditures in Capitalist and Communist Nations* (Homewood: Irwin, 1968).
4. For an elaborate catalogue of such contexts in which the exchange theory can possibly be applied, see Sidney R. Waldman, "Exchange Theory and Political Analysis", in Andrew Effrat (ed), *Perspectives in Political Sociology* (Indianapolis: Bobbs-Merril, 1972).
5. Richard D. McKelvey, "Intransitivities in Multidimensional Voting Models and Some Implication for Agenda Control", *Journal of Economic Theory*, 12, 1976.

APPENDICES

APPENDIX A

LIST OF VARIABLES

V1: Changes in the direct transfers to the households in the governmental expenditures.

V2: Changes in the direct taxes in the governmental revenues.

V3: Changes in the size of the incumbent coalition.

V4: Turnover of the incumbent coalition.

V5: The rate of economic growth.

V6: The rate of population growth.

V7: The rate of inflation.

V8: The extent of the openness of the economy.

V9: Ideology of the incumbent coalition.

V10: Frequency of election.

V11: Minority support in the legislature.

V12: Federal structure of the government.

NOTE: For the sources of data and the measurement or coding of the variables, see chapter 3.

APPENDIX B

THE DATA

OBS/EL	V1	V2	V3	V4	V5	V6	V7	V8	V9	V10	V11	V12
ASTL55	11.29	7.19	0.7	1	3.7	2.3	4.3	38.8	1	.72	0	1
ASTL58	3.78	6.45	1.3	1	3.7	2.3	4.3	38.8	1	.72	0	1
ASTL61	0.33	1.30	4.4	1	5.9	2.0	2.7	32.3	1	.72	0	1
ASTL63	3.32	0.32	4.0	1	5.9	2.0	2.7	32.3	1	.72	0	1
ASTL66	1.06	2.82	3.9	1	5.9	2.0	2.7	32.3	1	.72	0	1
ASTL69	11.07	3.04	6.5	1	5.9	2.0	2.7	32.3	1	.72	0	1
ASTL72	10.67	5.33	6.2	3	3.4	2.0	15.5	31.7	3	.72	0	1
ASTL75	2.32	7.22	1.3	3	3.4	2.0	15.5	31.7	1	.72	0	1
ASTL77	1.82	1.39	2.8	1	3.4	2.0	15.5	31.7	1	.72	0	1
ASTR53	12.80	3.95	5.9	1	5.8	0.2	3.3	42.6	2	.56	0	1
ASTR56	1.25	1.34	5.6	1	5.8	0.2	3.3	42.6	2	.56	0	1
ASTR59	0.99	2.46	0.0	1	5.8	0.2	3.3	42.6	2	.56	0	1
ASTR62	0.58	1.87	0.4	1	4.5	0.6	3.9	51.6	2	.56	0	1
ASTR66	11.17	13.97	41.0	2	4.5	0.6	3.9	51.6	1	.56	0	1
ASTR71	8.05	4.24	1.7	3	4.3	0.2	8.4	68.1	3	.56	0	1
ASTR75	1.13	1.42	0.4	1	4.3	0.2	8.4	68.1	3	.56	0	1
BELG54	11.28	8.35	1.7	3	2.6	0.6	1.4	63.1	2	.32	0	0
BELG58	8.57	8.99	8.2	2	2.6	0.6	1.4	63.1	1	.32	0	0
BELG61	14.48	12.12	20.6	2	4.7	0.5	3.6	72.6	2	.32	0	0
BELG65	2.04	1.91	15.6	1	4.7	0.5	3.6	72.6	2	.32	0	0
BELG68	2.78	1.36	2.8	1	4.7	0.5	3.6	72.6	2	.32	0	0
BELG71	20.71	16.83	2.5	1	3.2	0.4	10.4	96.0	2	.32	0	0

(Contd.)

THE DATA – *Contd.*

OBS/EL	V1	V2	V3	V4	V5	V6	V7	V8	V9	V10	V11	V12
BELG74	10.07	17.93	9.5	3	3.2	0.4	10.4	96.0	1	.32	1	0
BELG78	21.45	*	13.1	2	3.2	0.4	10.4	96.0	2	.32	1	0
CANA53	1.63	*	0.7	1	3.7	2.7	1.5	42.2	3	.36	0	1
CANA58	6.75	19.62	4.8	3	3.7	2.7	1.5	42.2	1	.36	0	1
CANA63	18.05	13.59	11.9	3	5.6	1.8	3.2	39.1	3	.36	1	1
CANA65	1.34	11.33	1.5	1	5.6	1.8	3.2	39.1	3	.36	1	1
CANA68	0.75	6.75	5.3	1	5.6	1.8	3.2	39.1	3	.36	0	1
CANA72	15.30	3.96	7.0	1	4.2	1.4	10.0	47.4	3	.36	1	1
CANA74	3.00	14.60	4.7	1	4.2	1.4	10.0	47.4	3	.36	0	1
COST70	15.41	8.15	6.0	3	6.1	2.8	14.6	67.4	3	.30	0	0
COST74	19.00	10.04	12.4	1	6.1	2.8	14.6	67.4	3	.30	1	0
COST78	21.30	4.71	0.3	3	6.1	2.8	14.6	67.4	1	.30	1	0
DENM60	16.50	1.41	4.6	2	4.7	0.7	6.3	61.9	2	.52	1	0
DENM64	18.10	7.96	6.0	2	4.7	0.7	6.3	61.9	3	.52	1	0
DENM66	17.50	5.52	3.6	1	4.7	0.7	6.3	61.9	3	.52	1	0
DENM73	25.30	8.69	6.2	3	2.8	0.4	13.5	59.8	2	.52	1	0
DENM75	6.70	1.13	3.8	2	2.8	0.4	13.5	59.8	2	.52	1	0
FINL54	10.93	0.17	7.1	2	4.0	1.0	2.5	46.6	3	.40	0	0
FINL62	5.55	3.55	4.9	2	4.6	0.4	2.7	43.9	2	.40	0	0
FINL66	5.91	15.79	17.0	2	4.6	0.4	2.7	43.9	3	.40	0	0
FINL70	1.24	8.23	9.4	1	4.8	0.2	18.0	55.7	3	.40	0	0
FINL72	7.61	1.43	10.0	1	4.8	0.2	18.0	55.7	2	.40	0	0

(Contd.)

THE DATA – *Contd.*

OBS/EL	V1	V2	V3	V4	V5	V6	V7	V8	V9	V10	V11	V12
FINL75	1.47	1.01	1.0	1	4.8	0.2	18.0	55.7	2	.40	0	0
FRAN65	4.05	3.89	2.7	1	5.5	1.0	4.0	27.2	1	.55	0	0
FRAN69	0.63	1.27	0.3	1	5.5	1.0	4.0	27.2	1	.55	0	0
FRAN74	2.27	2.80	11.4	2	3.7	0.9	12.5	38.7	1	.55	1	0
GERM53	18.30	1.03	17.0	2	7.3	1.0	1.5	36.7	1	.36	0	1
GERM57	14.81	1.60	10.3	2	7.3	1.0	1.5	36.7	1	.36	0	1
GERM61	8.02	10.98	4.5	2	4.4	0.9	2.7	36.0	1	.36	0	1
GERM65	1.83	1.46	1.0	1	4.4	0.9	2.7	36.0	1	.36	0	1
GERM69	8.46	11.05	31.7	2	4.4	0.9	2.7	36.0	2	.36	0	1
GERM72	1.11	16.10	34.6	2	2.6	0.2	6.3	45.4	2	.36	0	1
GERM76	1.33	4.71	3.7	1	2.6	0.2	6.3	45.4	2	.36	0	1
INDI62	11.20	6.33	1.8	1	3.7	2.4	10.0	12.0	2	.48	0	1
INDI67	1.11	10.52	5.3	1	3.7	2.4	10.0	12.0	2	.48	0	1
INDI71	12.00	13.76	3.0	1	3.6	2.5	9.9	12.3	2	.48	0	1
INDI77	15.03	19.48	0.7	3	3.6	2.5	9.9	12.3	1	.48	0	1
IREL54	1.09	14.71	0.9	3	0.9	0.5	3.8	40.8	2	.60	0	0
IREL57	1.43	10.72	1.1	3	0.9	0.5	3.8	70.8	1	.60	0	0
IREL61	17.58	2.26	4.5	1	4.2	0.4	5.7	76.9	1	.60	1	0
IREL65	4.62	8.87	3.9	1	4.2	0.4	5.7	76.9	1	.60	0	0
IREL69	1.76	1.43	2.0	1	4.2	0.4	5.7	76.9	1	.60	0	0
IREL73	11.32	10.64	3.1	3	3.9	1.1	21.1	97.2	2	.60	0	0
IREL77	19.49	*	1.8	3	3.9	1.1	21.1	97.2	1	.36	0	0

(Contd.)

THE DATA – *Contd.*

OBS/EL	V1	V2	V3	V4	V5	V6	V7	V8	V9	V10	V11	V12
ITAL53	11.31	9.75	14.7	2	5.7	0.7	2.4	26.0	1	.36	1	0
ITAL58	16.32	9.48	6.9	2	5.7	0.7	2.4	26.0	2	.36	1	0
ITAL63	12.22	1.80	12.5	2	5.8	0.6	4.3	32.0	2	.36	0	0
ITAL68	22.82	2.79	20.4	2	5.8	0.6	4.3	32.0	1	.36	1	0
ITAL72	14.73	5.59	8.7	2	2.9	0.5	20.6	45.1	2	.36	0	0
ITAL76	20.91	10.12	9.1	2	2.9	0.5	20.6	45.1	1	.36	1	0
JAPA55	2.80	2.25	24.3	2	8.3	1.2	2.6	25.5	1	.72	0	0
JAPA58	4.67	1.55	5.4	1	8.3	1.2	2.6	25.5	1	.72	0	0
JAPA60	2.18	1.54	0.2	1	10.4	1.0	6.3	18.9	1	.72	0	0
JAPA63	12.23	0.07	3.7	1	10.4	1.0	6.3	18.9	1	.72	0	0
JAPA67	13.93	1.82	5.1	1	10.4	1.0	6.3	18.9	1	.72	0	0
JAPA69	1.00	0.97	1.4	1	10.4	1.0	6.3	18.1	1	.72	0	0
JAPA72	2.16	0.88	0.5	1	4.6	1.2	13.9	23.2	1	.72	0	0
JAPA76	7.12	4.38	5.1	1	4.6	1.2	13.9	23.2	1	.72	1	0
NETH59	14.17	5.59	21.4	2	4.6	1.3	2.4	95.6	1	.44	0	0
NETH63	12.17	1.24	1.8	1	5.3	1.3	5.2	91.9	1	.44	0	0
NETH67	8.70	0.97	4.3	1	5.3	1.3	5.2	91.9	1	.44	0	0
NETH72	13.00	11.27	7.6	2	3.1	0.8	10.4	99.1	2	.44	0	0
NETH77	14.41	14.22	13.0	2	3.1	0.8	10.4	99.1	1	.44	0	0
NEWZ57	10.33	3.68	4.0	3	4.1	2.2	4.3	59.4	3	.36	0	0
NEWZ60	7.76	11.51	0.7	3	2.0	1.7	4.4	46.3	1	.36	0	0
NEWZ63	1.60	1.57	0.5	1	2.0	1.7	4.4	46.3	1	.36	0	0

(Contd.)

THE DATA – *Contd.*

OBS/EL	V1	V2	V3	V4	V5	V6	V7	V8	V9	V10	V11	V12
NEWZ66	3.98	5.09	3.5	1	2.0	1.7	4.4	46.3	1	.36	0	0
NEWZ69	1.21	0.65	1.8	1	2.0	1.7	4.4	46.3	1	.36	0	0
NEWZ72	9.43	5.83	3.2	3	2.1	1.5	18.0	52.7	3	.36	0	0
NEWZ75	4.37	9.57	1.2	3	2.1	1.5	18.0	52.7	1	.36	0	0
NORW53	12.67	5.80	1.0	1	3.3	0.9	3.8	85.0	3	.28	0	0
NORW57	11.36	6.22	1.6	1	3.3	0.9	3.8	85.0	3	.28	0	0
NORW61	10.67	19.57	1.5	1	4.9	0.8	4.4	81.9	3	.28	1	0
NORW65	20.22	15.23	0.9	3	4.9	0.8	4.4	81.9	1	.28	1	0
NORW69	15.45	4.23	2.7	1	4.9	0.8	4.4	81.9	1	.28	1	0
NORW73	15.87	17.35	10.0	3	4.5	0.7	11.5	87.6	3	.28	1	0
NORW77	12.07	9.78	11.5	2	4.5	0.7	11.5	87.6	3	.28	1	0
SRIL56	13.39	7.18	3.4	3	3.0	2.5	0.6	72.1	3	.24	0	0
SRIL60	13.77	13.98	7.1	3	5.7	2.4	3.4	47.9	3	.24	1	0
SRIL65	15.85	16.05	13.5	3	5.7	2.4	3.4	47.9	1	.24	0	0
SRIL70	20.00	2.82	1.9	3	5.8	2.1	8.1	59.3	3	.24	0	0
SWED58	11.67	5.50	7.9	2	3.4	0.6	3.5	55.0	3	.36	1	0
SWED60	12.12	6.95	1.6	1	4.1	0.7	4.7	44.1	3	.36	1	0
SWED64	1.05	1.58	0.5	1	4.1	0.7	4.7	44.1	3	.36	1	0
SWED68	0.78	2.50	2.8	1	4.1	0.7	4.7	44.1	3	.36	0	0
SWED70	3.46	6.41	4.8	1	1.3	0.6	12.3	54.7	3	.36	1	0
SWED73	4.83	11.93	1.7	1	1.3	0.6	12.3	54.7	3	.36	1	0
SWED76	2.13	19.32	7.2	3	1.3	0.6	12.3	54.7	1	.36	0	0

(*Contd.*)

THE DATA – *Contd.*

OBS/EL	V1	V2	V3	V4	V5	V6	V7	V8	V9	V10	V11	V12
UKIN55	4.65	10.41	1.7	1	2.6	0.4	3.9	43.9	1	.36	0	0
UKIN59	1.00	1.32	0.3	1	2.6	0.4	3.9	43.9	1	.36	0	0
UKIN64	9.57	1.22	5.3	3	2.9	0.5	4.6	41.6	3	.36	0	0
UKIN66	0.87	0.81	3.9	1	2.9	0.5	4.6	41.6	3	.36	0	0
UKIN70	7.49	4.93	1.4	3	2.1	0.4	21.3	53.9	1	.36	0	0
UKIN74	4.41	8.56	7.3	3	2.1	0.4	21.3	53.9	3	.36	0	0
USAM52	9.84	11.75	5.5	3	2.8	1.7	1.5	9.1	1	.48	0	1
USAM56	1.82	5.40	2.3	1	2.8	1.7	1.5	9.1	1	.48	0	1
USAM60	1.71	1.63	7.7	3	4.4	1.3	3.2	9.4	3	.48	0	1
USAM64	4.00	8.64	11.4	1	4.4	1.3	3.2	9.4	3	.48	0	1
USAM68	15.42	13.89	17.7	3	4.4	1.3	3.2	9.4	1	.48	0	1
USAM72	12.31	5.72	17.3	1	3.2	0.9	8.5	15.4	1	.48	0	1
USAM76	14.04	3.58	10.6	3	3.2	0.9	8.5	15.4	3	.48	0	1
VENE63	19.77	15.71	15.5	1	5.9	3.2	1.0	58.0	3	.25	0	1
VENE68	13.59	18.84	3.6	3	5.9	3.2	1.3	50.4	1	.25	1	1
VENE73	15.56	15.51	19.6	3	5.5	2.9	8.0	54.2	3	.25	0	1

* Data not available.

APPENDIX C

CORRELATION MATRIX OF THE VARIABLES

	V1	V2*	V3	V4	V5	V6	V7	V8	V9	V10	V11	V12
V1	1.0											
V2	.29	1.0										
V3	.24	.26	1.0									
V4	.37	.44	.16	1.0								
V5	.15	–.25	.13	–.24	1.0							
V6	.14	.22	–.08	.14	.19	1.0						
V7	.12	.04	–.11	.21	–.27	–.11	1.0					
V8	.30	.20	–.03	.15	–.25	–.24	.19	1.0				
V9	.07	.09	.01	.05	.01	–.01	.08	.15	1.0			
V10	–.31	–.39	–.15	–.24	–.28	–.03	.06	–.17	–.39	1.0		
V11	.41	.17	.01	.07	.01	–.09	.11	.20	.18	–.24	1.0	
V12	–.16	.10	.14	–.08	.08	.37	–.24	–.48	.01	.22	–.26	1.0

* N= 123 only; for the rest of the variables, N= 126.

NOTE: For the explanations of the variables, see Appendix A.

APPENDIX D

MEAN, STANDARD DEVIATION, MINIMUM AND MAXIMUM VALUES OF THE VARIABLES

	Mean	Std. Dev.	Minimum	Maximum
V1	8.96	6.56	0.33	25.30
V2*	6.97	5.48	0.07	19.62
V3	6.57	7.07	0	41.00
V4	1.77	0.86	1	3
V5	4.37	1.81	0.90	10.40
V6	1.15	0.80	0.20	3.90
V7	7.14	5.42	0.60	21.30
V8	49.85	23.36	9.10	99.10
V9	1.86	0.87	1	3
V10	0.44	0.14	0.24	0.72
V11	0.25	0.48	0	1
V12	0.35	0.48	0	1

* N = 123 only; for the rest of the variables, N = 126.

NOTE: For the explanation of the variables, see Appendix A.

BIBLIOGRAPHY

Almond, Gabriel and G. Bingham Powell, Jr., *Comparative Politics: System, Process and Policy* (Boston: Little, Brown, 1978).

Anderson, Charles W., "System and Strategy in Comparative Policy Analysis: A Plea for Contextual and Experiential Knowledge", in William B. Gwyn and George C. Edwards (eds), *Perspectives in Public Policy Making* (New Orleans: Tulane University, 1975).

Ashford, Douglas (ed), *Comparing Public Policies: New Concepts and Methods*. (Beverly Hills: Sage, 1978).

Becker, Gary S., *The Economic Approach to Human Behavior* (Chicago: The Univ. of Chicago Press, 1976).

Bell, Daniel, *The End of Ideology* (Glencoe: Free Press, 1960).

Bell, Daniel, *The Coming of Post-Industrial Society* (New York: Basic Books, 1973).

Benjamin, Roger, *The Limits of Politics: Collective Goods and Political Change in Post-Industrial Societies* (Chicago: Univ. of Chicago Press, 1980).

Bergstrom, T.C. and R.P. Goodman, "Private Demand for Public Goods", *American Economic Review,* 63, 1973.

Birdsell, Richard, "A Study of the Demand for Public Good" in Richard Musgrave (ed), *Essays in Fiscal Federalism* (Washington, D.C. : The Brookings Institution, 1965).

Blair, John P. and Steven M. Maser, "A Reassessment of

Axiomatic Models in Policy Studies", in Gordon Tullock and Richard E. Wagner (ed), *Policy Analysis and Deductive Reasoning* (Lexington: D.C. Heath, 1978).

Blau, Peter M., *Exchange and Power in Social Life* (New York: Wiley, 1964).

Borcherding, T.E. and R.T. Deacon, "The Demand for Services of Non-Federal Governments", *American Economic Review,* 62, 1972.

Boulter, Douglas R., "Setting Speed Limits ..... and Comparing Public Policy Making", *Comparative Politics,* 13, 1980.

Bowen, Howard, *Towards Social Economy* (New York: Rinehart, 1948).

Breton, Albert, "A Theory of Demand For Public Goods", *Canadian Journal of Economics and Political Science,* Nov. 1966.

Breton, Albert, *The Economic Theory of Representative Government* (Chicago: Aldine, 1974).

Bunce, Valerie, *Do New Leaders Make A Difference? Executive Succession and Public Policy Under Capitalism and Socialism* (Princeton: Princeton Univ. Press, 1981).

Cameron, David R., "The Expansion of Public Economy: A Comparative Analysis", *American Political Science Review,* 72, 1978.

Castles, Francis G., "The Impact of Parties on Public Expenditure", in his edited, *The Impact of Parties: Politics and Policies in Democratic Capitalist States* (Beverly Hills: Sage, 1982).

Chadwick-Jones, J.K., *Social Exchange Theory: Its Structure and Influence in Social Psychology* (London: Academic Press, 1976).

Chamberlin, E.H., *Theory of Monopolistic Competition,* 8th Ed. (Cambridge: Harvard Univ. Press, 1962).

Cnudde, Charles F. and Donald J. McCrone, "Party Competition and Welfare Policies in the American States", *American Political Science Review,* 63, 1969.

Curry, R.L., Jr. and L.L. Wade, *A Theory of Political Exchange: Economic Reasoning in Political Analysis* (Englewood Cliffs: Prentice-Hall, 1968).

Cyr, Arthur and Peter deLeon, "Comparative Policy Analysis", *Policy Sciences,* 6, 1975.

Davis, Otto A., M.A.H. Dempster and Aaron Wildavsky, "Towards a Predictive Theory of Budgetary Process", *British Journal of Political Science,* 4, 1974.

Dawson, Richard E. and James A. Robinson, "Inter-Party Competition, Economic Variables and Welfare Policies in American States", *Journal of Politics,* 25, 1963.

Day, Alan J. and Henry W. Degenhardt, *Political Parties in the World* (Essex: Longman, 1980).

Downs, Anthony, *An Economic Theory of Democracy* (New York: Harper and Row, 1957).

Dye, Thomas, *Politics, Economics and the Public: Policy Outcomes in American States* (Chicago: Rand McNally, 1966).

Feldman, Elliot J., "Comparative Public Policy: Field or Method?", *Comparative Politics,* 10, 1978.

Fenton, John H., *People and Parties in Politics* (New York: Scott, Foresman, 1966).

Fiorina, M.P. and R.G. Noll, "Voters, Bureaucrats and Legislators: A Rational Choice Perspective on the Growth of Bureaucracy", *Journal of Public Economics,* 7, 1978.

Galbraith, J.K., *The New Industrial State* (London: Harrish Hamilton, 1967).

Hancock, M. Donald, "Comparative Public Policy: An Assessment", in Ada W. Finifter (ed), *Political Science: The State of the Discipline* (Washington, D.C.: APSA, 1983).

Hansen, Susan B., "Public Policy Analysis: Some Recent Developments and Current Problems", in Ada W. Finifter (ed), *Political Science: The State of the Discipline.* (Washington, D.C.: APSA, 1983).

Hartle, Douglas, *Theory of Budgetary Expenditures* (Toronto: Univ. of Toronto Press, 1976).

Heath, Anthony, *Rational Choice and Social Exchange* (Cambridge: Cambridge Univ. Press, 1976).

Heclo, Hugh, *Modern Social Politics in Britain and Sweden* (New Haven: Yale Univ. Press, 1974)

Hempel, Carl G., *Philosophy of Natural Science* (Englewood Cliffs: Prentice-Hall, 1966).

Herman, Valentine and John Pope, "Minority Governments in Western Democracies", *British Journal of Political Science*, 3, 1973.

Hibbs, Douglas A., Jr., "Political Parties and Macroeconomic Policy, *American Political Science Review,* 71, 1977.

Higley, John and Gwen Moore, "Elite Integration in the United States and Australia", *American Political Science Review,* 75, 1981.

Holt, Robert T. and John M. Richardson, Jr., "Competing Paradigms in Comparative Politics", in Holt and Turner (eds), *The Methodology of Comparative Research* (New York: Free Press, 1970).

Homans, George C. *Social Behavior: Its Elementary Forms* (New York: Harcourt, Brace, 1961).

Huntington, Samuel P., *Political Order in Changing Societies* (New Haven: Yale Univ. Press, 1968).

Inman, Robert P., "Testing Political Economy's 'as if' Proposition: Is the Median Income Voter Really Decisive?", *Public Choice,* 33, 1978.

Jackman, Robert W., *Politics and Social Equality* (New York: John Wiley, 1975).

Jennings, Edward T., "Competition, Constituencies and Welfare policies in American States", *American Political Science Review,* 73, 1979.

Kerr, Clark, *et al., Industrialism and Industrial Man* (Cambridge: Harvard Univ. Press, 1960).

Key, V.O., Jr., *Southern Politics* (New York: Knopf, 1949).

King, Anthony, "Ideas, Institutions and the Policies of Governments: A Comparative Analysis", *British Journal of Political Science,* 3, 1973.

Kramer, Gerald H., "Short-term Fluctuations in U.S. Voting Behavior, 1896-1964", *American Political Science Review,* 65, 1971.

Kuhn, Thomas S., *The Structure of Scientific Revolution* (Chicago: Univ. of Chicago Press, 1964).

Lasch, Christopher, "Towards a Theory of Post-Industrial Society" in M. Donald Hancock and Gideon Sjoberg (eds), *Politics in the Post-Welfare State* (New York: Columbia Univ. Press, 1972).

Lehmbruch, Gerhard, "Introduction: Neo-Corporatism in Comparative Perspective", in Lehmbruch and Schmitter (eds), *Patterns of Corporatist Policy Making* (Beverly Hills: Sage, 1982).

Leichter, Howard M., "Comparative Public Policy: Problems and Prospects", *Policy Studies Journal,* 5, 1977.

Lenski, Gerhard, *Power and Privilege: A Theory of Social Stratification* (New York: McGraw-Hill, 1966).

Lindblom, Charles E., *The Intelligence of Democracy* (New York: Free Press, 1965).

Lipset, Seymour Martin, *Political Man* (Garden City: Doubleday, 1980).

Loewenberg, Gerhard and Samuel C. Patterson, *Comparing Legislatures* (London: Oxford Univ. Press, 1979).

Mackie, Thomas and Richard Rose, *The International Almanac of Electoral History*, 2nd Ed. (New York: Free Press, 1982).

McKelvey, Richard D., "Intransitivities in Multidimensional Voting Models and Some Implications for Agenda Control", *Journal of Economic Theory,* 12, 1976.

Mitchell, William C., "The Shape of Political Theory to Come: From Political Sociology to Political Economy", *American Behavioral Scientist*, 11, 1967.

Niskanen, William, *Bureaucracy and Representative Government* (Chicago: Aldine, 1971).

Nordhaus, William D., "The Political Business Cycle", *Review of Economic Studies,* 42, 1975.

Olson, Mancur, Jr., "Rapid Growth as a Destabilizing Force", *Journal of Economic History,* 23, 1963.

Organization for Economic Cooperation and Development, *National Accounts of OECD Countries* (various volumes).

Peltzman, Sam, "Towards a More General Theory of Regulation", *Journal of Law and Economics,* 19, 1976.

Peters, B. Guy, "Developments in Comparative Policy Studies: A Brief Review", *Policy Studies Journal,* 5, 1977.

Powell, G. Bingham, Jr., *Contemporary Democracies: Participation, Stability and Violence* (Cambridge: Harvard Univ. Press, 1982).

Pryor, Frederick, *Public Expenditures in Capitalist and Communist Nations* (Homewood: Irwin, 1968).

Riker, William H., "Federalism", in Fred I. Greenstein and Nelson W. Polsby (eds), *Handbook of Political Science,* Vol. 5 (Reading: Addison-Wesley, 1975).

Riker, William H., "Implications from Disequilibrium of

Majority Rule for the Study of Institutions" in Ordeshook and Shepsle (eds), *Political Equilibrium* (Boston: Kluwar-Nijhoff, 1982).

Riker, William H. and Peter C. Ordeshook, *An Introduction to Positive Political Theory* (Englewood Cliffs: Prentice-Hall, 1973).

Robinson, Joan, *The Economics of Imperfect Competition* (London: Macmillan, 1961).

Romer, T. and H. Rosenthal, "Political Resource Allocation, Cotrolled Agendas and Status-quo", *Public Choice,* 33, 1978.

Rose, Richard, "Comparing Public Policy: An Overview", *European Journal of Political Research,* 1, 1973.

Schmidt, Manfred G., "The Role of Parties in Shaping Macroeconomic Policy", in Castles (ed), *The Impact of Parties: Politics and Policies in Democratic Capitalist States* (Beverly Hills: Sage, 1982).

Schmitter, Philippe C., "Modes of Interest Intermediation and Model of Societal Change in Western Europe", *Comparative Political Studies,* 10, 1977.

Sharkansky, I. and R. Hofferbert, "Dimensions of State Politics, Economics and Public Policy", *American Political Science Review,* 63, 1969.

Simmel, Georg, *The Sociology of Georg Simmel,* translated and edited by K.H. Wolff (New York: Free Press, 1950).

Stonecash, Jeff, "Politics, Wealth and Public Policy: The Significance of Political System", in Thomas R. Dye and Virginia Gray (eds), *The Determinants of Public Policy* (Lexington: D.C. Heath, 1980).

Taylor, Charles Lewis and David A. Jodice, *World Handbook of Political and Social Indicators,* 3rd Ed. (New Haven: Yale Univ. Press, 1983).

Thibaut, J.W. and H.H. Kelly, *The Social Psychology of*

Groups (New York: Wiley, 1959).

Touraine, Alan, *The Post-Industrial Society* (New York: Random House, 1971).

Tufte, Edward, "Determinants of the Outcome of Midterm Congressional Elections", *American Political Science Review,* 69, 1975.

Tufte, Edward, *Political Control of Economy* (Princeton: Princeton Univ. Press, 1978).

United Nations, *Statistical Yearbook* (various volumes).

United Nations, *Yearbook of National Accounts Statistics* (various volumes).

Van den Doel, Hans, *Democracy and Welfare Economics* (Cambridge: Cambridge Univ. Press, 1979).

Wade, L.L. and R.L. Curry, Jr., *A Logic of Public Policy: Aspects of Political Economy* (Belmont: Wadsworth, 1970).

Waldman, Sidney R., "Exchange Theory and Political Analysis", in Andrew Effrat (ed), *Perspectives in Political Sociology* (Indianapolis: Bobbs-Merrill, 1972).

Wheare, K.C., *Legislatures* (London: Oxford Univ. Press, 1963).

Wildavsky, Aaron, *The Politics of Budgetary Process* (Boston: Little, Brown, 1974).

Wilensky, Harold, *The Welfare State and Equality* (Berkeley: Univ. of California Press, 1975).

Wilensky, Harold, *The 'New Corporatism', Centralization and the Welfare State* (Beverly Hills: Sage, 1976).

Williams, Bruce A., "Organizational Determinants of Policy Change", in Thomas R. Dye and Virginia Gray (eds), *The Determinants of Public Policy* (Lexington: D.C. Heath, 1980).

Winters, Richard, "Party Control and Policy Change", *American Journal of Political Science,* 20, 1976.

Monopolistic political competition, 21, 28, 84
Multiple Regress analysis, 66-68

New incombent party, 48
Null hypothesis, 70, 71

Observations, 57
Old incombent party, 48
Opposition, conditions of, 47
Organizational constraints, 86

Paradigm, 17
Pension payments, 56
Policy-benefit functions, 37, 39, 40, 43
Policy changes, 62-64
Policy cost functions, 39-43
Policy determinants, 10-11; conception of, 19
Policy-opposition functions, 43-44
Policy out-put change, 49
Political actors, 18
Political business cycles, 64-65
Political environment matters, 11-12, 62, 84; variables, 75
Political exchange, 10, 17, 18, 55, 73; process of, 18, 87-88; nature of, 34-35
Political institutionalization, 11
Political market, characterization of, 31
Population growth, impact of, 60; rate of, 70
Preliminary assumption, 32-33
Profit seeking monopology, 36
Pryor, Fredrick, 86
Public expenditure, 59
Public policy, determinants of, 21-22; economic determinants of, 13-14; implementation of, 12-13; pattern of, 14, 33; output of, 36-37, 42

Rational choice approach, 20-22, 84
Redistributive policies, 73
Re-election, probability of, 32, 42

Sickness benefits, 56
Social security payments, 56
Socio-economic factors, 58-59
State political systems, 11-12
Supply restriction, 29
System demand curve, 47

Transfers, proportion of, 71, 72

Unemployment allowance, 33; benefit, 50, 59-62

Variables, 91; correlation matrix of, 97
Veteran benefits, 56

Wade, L. L., 15
Welfare expenditure, 56
West Germany, 29
Wilensky, Harold, 13, 59

Index

Acid rain, 35
Administration, 64
American state policies, 13
Ashford, Douglas, 11, 12

Beneficiaries, 34, 49, 84
Bridge principles, 84
Budget constraints, 36
Bunce, Valerie, 86
Bureaucratic organization, impact of, 12

Cameron, David R., 61
Castles, Francis G., 85
Changes in Transfers, 66-67
Coalition, 31, 51
Comparative politics, 10
Competing paradigms, 10
Constraints, 14, 17, 31, 60
Corporatism, 11
Cross-national empirical analysis, 54-74; test, 51, 54
Curry, R.L., 15

Data, 91-96
Davis, Otto A., 63
Democratic political system, 9, 19, 54, 75
Dependent variables, 56-57, 84
Direct taxes, 70, 73; proportion of, 73
Downs, Anthony, 32
Dual economies, 60

Economic concession, 59
Economic environmental variables, 84-85; exchange, 19; growth rate of, 69; market, 54
Economic Resource model, 12-13

Election, 31, 28, 35, 48; frequency of, 86
Empirical data, 22
Employment, 30
Environmental factors, 54

Governmental expenditures, 56
Government's involvement, 47; policy, 16
Green Party, 29

Hempel, Carl G., 83
Hibbs, Douglas A., 85
Hypothetical policy, 38

Incumbent coalition, 57-58
Incombent Party's policy, 35, 42, 85
Individual choice, 36
Inflation, high rates of, 61
Internal principles, 83

Jackman, Robert W., 63
Japan, 70
Job training, 63

Key, V.O., 11
Kuhn, Thomas S., 10

Labour force, 54
Long run, policy output in, 47-48

Manifestoes, 33
Marginal change, 50
Marginal Opposition (MO), 43
Marginal support, 43, 44
Median voter's benefit, 37-38, 49, 87
Monopoly market, 31, 33